W9-BUG-764

STRENGTH IN NUMBERS

STRENGTH IN NUMBERS

How Polls Work and
Why We Need Them

G. ELLIOTT MORRIS

W. W. NORTON & COMPANY
Independent Publishers Since 1923

Copyright © 2022 by G. Elliott Morris

All rights reserved
Printed in the United States of America
First Edition

For information about permission to reproduce selections from this book, write to
Permissions, W. W. Norton & Company, Inc., 500 Fifth Avenue, New York, NY 10110

For information about special discounts for bulk purchases, please contact
W. W. Norton Special Sales at specialsales@wwnorton.com or 800-233-4830

Manufacturing by Lake Book Manufacturing
Production manager: Beth Steidle

ISBN 978-0-393-86697-1

W. W. Norton & Company, Inc., 500 Fifth Avenue, New York, N.Y. 10110
www.wwnorton.com

W. W. Norton & Company Ltd., 15 Carlisle Street, London W1D 3BS

1 2 3 4 5 6 7 8 9 0

Did you, too, O friend, suppose democracy was only for elections, for politics, and for a party name? I say democracy is only of use there that it may pass on and come to its flower and fruit in manners, in the highest forms of interaction between people, and their beliefs—in religion, literature, colleges and schools—democracy in all public and private life.

—WALT WHITMAN, *DEMOCRATIC VISTAS*, 1871

CONTENTS

INTRODUCTION

I f you have heard anything about public opinion polling, it is probably about the industry's failures. The popular retellings of history hold
that polls were wrong in their first major test in 1948, when George
Gallup and other pollsters declared that incumbent president Harry Truman would lose to Thomas Dewey (in reality, Dewey didn't even come
close), and that they have been wrong many times since. Take the results
of the 2016 election. On average, polls predicted that Hillary Clinton
would win the popular vote by three or four percentage points, and the
Electoral College by over 100 votes. A new generation of data-driven polling experts gave forecasts with precise, mathematical confidence in her
victory. But she lost in five key states where the polls consistently had her
leading, and only wound up winning the popular vote by two points. The
press and the public derided polls, and the pollsters, as inaccurate, misleading, and increasingly irrelevant.

The 2020 election was supposed to be the year that polls came back.
Pollsters had learned from their mistakes and fixed—or so some said—the
methodological problems that caused them to underestimate the number
of Donald Trump's supporters in the electorate. Statistical forecasting
models predicted a landslide victory for Joe Biden. Instead, the election

was so razor-thin in several states, and ballot-counting so slow due to a surge in mail-in voting and other disruptions caused by the covid-19 pandemic, that the contest wasn't called by major media networks for four days. The official post-election analysis from the American Association for Public Opinion Research (AAPOR), the United States' association of pollsters, said the miss constituted the industry's worst performance since 1980.

It looks like the polls, despite nearly a century of trial, error, scientific innovation, and constant promises of improvement, are just hopelessly broken. Right?

Perhaps not.

A PROBLEM OF POLLING, AND OF POLL-WATCHING

We are not just misreading the polls, but also missing their larger promise for our politics. On the first and more narrow count, the evidence shows us that public opinion surveys (which I use interchangeably with "polls" throughout this book to refer to questionnaires eliciting responses from a group of people) are not capable of providing laser-like predictions of election outcomes. Rather than suggesting a surefire loss for Donald Trump in 2016, the polling data, if analyzed properly, suggested that there was a much higher chance of his victory than most reporters and television news pundits thought. Instead of relying too heavily on these polls, the media may have erred by not relying on them enough—and by incorrectly interpreting the polling data when it did. More than anything, the media and public believed in polls too much and in the wrong ways. And many repeated these mistakes in 2020.

In fact, polls are only a tad worse on average than they have been historically—and much better than the forecasts generated during the industry's infancy. At a conference at the University of Iowa in 1949, George Gallup, the founding figure in modern American polling, reported that the major pollsters had issued 446 forecasts of candidates' vote shares in elections covering the preceding fourteen years. Those predictions missed each party's vote share by an average of four percentage points—eight points when expressed as the miss on the winning candidate's margin, as it is commonly expressed today—a fact that Gallup said "marveled him." Given the complexity of human behavior and the number of variables that can impact an election outcome, he said, it was quite impressive that polls could come so close. These days, national polls miss the winning party's vote share an average of just one or two points in most elections. Even in 2020, they were only off by two and a half. Few other indicators have such a record of accuracy in measuring public opinion.

In 2018, the political scientists Will Jennings and Christopher Wlezien performed a study similar to Gallup's, but across a much broader range. They analyzed thousands of polls taken during 220 different elections across 32 countries from 1942 to 2017. Comparing the pre-election snapshots in these polls to the actual results of the election, they found that polls worldwide have not gotten less accurate over time. Rather, a longer view suggests that the recent blips experienced by the US polling industry are within the normal bounds of historical errors. "If anything," Jennings and Wlezien write, "polling errors are getting smaller on average.... [While] claims about the demise of pre-election polling have become common in recent times, we find little basis to support them."[1] Though the polls in 2020 were more biased than at any point in the past twenty years, they were better than they were ninety years ago.

It turns out, then, that polling has gotten a whole lot better over time. It's just hard for readers and reporters to see how, and where.

First and foremost, polls suffer from the problem that most people expect too much of them. This is not their fault; most citizens have been misled into believing that surveys are more like an assured statistical calculation than a rough estimate, such as a weather forecast; told that there's a 40% chance of rain, no one should be shocked that they're caught in a sudden downpour. Instead of calling winners and losers in a binary fashion (proclaiming that Clinton will win and Trump will lose in 2016, for example), polls calculate a range of possibilities for any given percentage (for example, saying that Clinton is favored to beat Trump, but she could just as easily win by five percentage points as lose by one).

Take a poll conducted by ABC News and the *Washington Post* in Wisconsin before the 2020 election. The survey suggested that Joe Biden, Donald Trump's Democratic rival, was 17 percentage points ahead of the incumbent president; 57% of the Wisconsin "likely voters" in their sample said they would support Biden, versus 40% for Trump. The news organizations reported that the "margin of error" for the poll was 4 percentage points for each candidate's vote share, meaning Joe Biden could be up by as much as 25 or as little as 9 points. After all the votes were tallied, Biden beat Trump among Wisconsinites by less than a percentage point, making the ABC/*Washington Post* poll 16 points off in the end—a result way outside the margin of error.

The "margin of error" is what pollsters call this range of possible outcomes. It provides critical information for consumers of political polls. It tells us how confident we can be in the poll's finding; how far away its estimates could be from reality purely because of random flukes in the way it was conducted.

But when it comes to modern polling, this "traditional" margin of sampling error is not enough. There are too many different types of errors that can push a poll off course, and the margin of error that pollsters typically report does not take all of them into account. In addition to random sampling error in who answers a poll, a survey can end up being biased by an inability to reach certain populations, by a higher rate of refusals among unwilling groups, by misleading or imprecise question wording, and by unavoidable random variation in the types of people answering it. In 2018, statisticians at Stanford, Microsoft, and Columbia University published an analysis of 4,221 polls taken from 608 state-level presidential, senatorial, and gubernatorial elections between 1998 and 2014 that found that the real margin of error for a poll is more than twice the size of the one most people hear reported. If poll-watchers had better understood the "true" margin of error in polls, they would not have been shocked by medium-sized errors. That would also make them less prone to thinking we should toss polls out altogether.[2]

There is no dancing around the troubling facts of polling. But a fair reckoning of the performance of polls, which is badly needed, must place blame both on the pollsters creating political surveys and the people consuming them. Fortunately, the evidence needed for this reckoning is already right before us. We simply need the right tools and outlook to comprehend its value.

IF YOU HATE THE POLLS, you are not alone. If you were a supporter of Hillary Clinton or Joe Biden, you probably feel the polls betrayed you, leading you into a false sense of comfort that left you surprised—maybe even distraught—two elections in a row. If you are instead a Republican or a political independent, you might believe polls are used to suppress the voices of people like you. If I were in any of your shoes, I would hate polls too.

Skepticism of the polls is entirely justified. In the past twenty years they have routinely underestimated the attitudes of conservative Americans, who often refuse when pollsters ask by phone or email to interview them. And while the polls on average are relatively unbiased, they are fantastically bad in some situations.

But part of the reason we're mad at polls is that there is a misunderstanding between the public and the pollsters—and between the pollsters and the press who cover their calculations. Many pollsters, with their fancy algorithms, "big data," call centers, and statistical wizardry, have done a poor job conveying the methods they use to arrive at their estimates and the conditions under which these estimates are invalidated. The press has done a poor job trying to understand these nuances, instead simply repeating misleading claims about too-narrow margins of error and hyping the ability of polls to predict the outcome of an electoral horse race. Very often, they are even more confident in the polls than the number-crunchers themselves. This skews the public's understanding of how polls work and how much they can really tell us about human behavior. Sometimes, a high level of confidence is warranted. But the people have not been given the chance to understand when that is the case.

Election forecasting—a practice I have engaged in—may also lead people astray. Forecasters take the polls, look at the historical deviation between averages and results on any given day in the election cycle, and explore the different paths the election could take going forward. But many forecasters are prone to underestimating the amount of potential error in the polls. In every presidential election year since 2012, for example, the bias in polls has grown larger, meaning election forecasts might overestimate the probability that the predicted winner will win.

WHAT YOU MISSED IN PUBLIC OPINION CLASS

The rush to declare polling dead is misguided. Polls are simultaneously better than we think and not up to the demands we make of them. Dismissing political surveys altogether would be outright dangerous. There is both a deep history and a recent record of polls fulfilling a key function in democratic societies. Though they are imperfect, polls shape the government's understanding of what the people want from their leaders. And, empirically, no other tool does such a good job taking the public's pulse.

"Issue polls" are where pollsters do most of their work, even though they tend to get lost in the sea of pre-election forecasts. They also more closely fulfill the original promise of the political poll: telling political leaders and elected officials what policies the people favor and what areas of American life the government is neglecting.

Good polls can reveal the will of the people. Condemning them as worthless is dangerous to this cause. In the abstract, polls are the key to social knowledge, what we know about ourselves as a collective. They are not only useful for electoral handicapping and as buttresses for newspaper headlines; they provide a voice for citizens, serving as a pipeline from the governed to the government and as a bulwark against despots. Polls give the people the ability to rein in their leaders between elections—but only if we can learn how to use them.

You don't have to look far to find concrete examples of polls serving meaningful functions in our electoral, judicial, and governing systems. In 2016, the Republican National Committee used polls to select candidates for their prime-time debates, elevating the status of those who had large followings and committing to obscurity those who did not. For their 2020 presidential primaries, the DNC followed suit. The Democrats also placed candidates with higher polling numbers at the center of the stage, assuring they were seen first and more often during the debate. With some imagination we can speculate how the world would be different if those decisions were made randomly.

Public opinion polls have also been instrumental in shaping Supreme Court decisions. When the Supreme Court in the 2013 case *Hollingsworth v. Perry* took up a challenge to a California law that prevented same-sex marriage, polling from Gallup showed marriage equality garnered only a bare majority of support from all American adults. At the time, the liberal justice Ruth Bader Ginsburg implied that a judicial solution on marriage at that moment could provoke a backlash to "momentum" that had been building for the cause, as she claimed the legalization of abortion under *Roe v. Wade* had done in the past.[3] By the time the Supreme Court granted same-sex couples the right to marry in *Obergefell v. Hodges* in 2015, 60% of the country supported it, according to Gallup's polling.[4] Justice Anthony Kennedy noted the trend in the majority opinion of the Court: "Judicial opinions addressing the issue have been informed by the contentions of parties and counsel, which, in turn, reflect the more general, societal discussion of same-sex marriage and its meaning that has occurred over the past decades. This has led to an enhanced understanding of the issue."

In another context, researchers have shown that if politicians know something is popular, they're more likely to vote for it. For instance, when the price of crude oil hit an all-time high in 2008, New Mexico found itself with a onetime surplus of nearly $400 million for the next fiscal year, since oil is one of the state's chief exports. A special session of the state's legislature was convened to decide how to spend it. These events created the perfect opportunity for political scientists Daniel Butler and David Nickerson to study the impacts that polls can have on legislators. They conducted a survey in every district of the state's House of Representatives to ask what voters wanted to do. On August 15, 2008—the day that New Mexico's special legislative session began—Butler and Nickerson mailed a letter to a random selection of 35 of the 70 representatives in the state's lower legislative chamber, telling them what their constituents wanted to do with the surplus. This allowed the scholars to compare the likelihood that a given representative would vote in favor of the position their voters desired on an upcoming bill for two groups of lawmakers: those who received the polling data, and those who did not. The results were clear: legislators who were given information about their constituents' views were more likely to do what they wanted.

The New Mexico legislature ended their special session by spending their surplus on infrastructure projects in part because legislators saw the polls that said voters wanted them to. Many of our elected representatives are on board with this model of governing. A congressman interviewed in the 1960s was quoted as saying: "That's the big problem. You're here to represent your people but you don't know what they want. The only way to really know is to take a referendum." He must not have heard about polling.[5]

THE CONVERSATION ABOUT POLLING in the media has focused far too much on how it has failed, and not enough on the more important matters at hand. Journalists, political commentators, and politicians have developed a poorly calibrated and shortsighted view of political polls in particular. Sadly, they have passed on these views to the public, whom polls are intended to empower in the first place.

In many cases, the denigration of polls is made by elites, elected officials, and ideological activists who have a stake in the public's voice not being heard. It is not a coincidence that the most fervent detractors of political surveys are those who have made their careers by wielding power over the masses; those who falsely proclaim to know the people better than they do themselves; or those who seek to abuse public opinion by artificially molding it in their favor and ignoring truer data.

Abandoning polling leaves the people worse off in the fight for democracy. In a world without polls, people will be left listening only to themselves and those closest to them, or to the loudest voices on television and social media. Neither are suitable replacements for the polls; both leave the public at risk of capture by those who would seek to raise or lower their pulse, not measure it.

Faced with the public's poor understanding of the margin of error, minimal awareness of the impact of issue polling, and an overconfident press, it might be tempting to look for a better technical solution. I could explain the formulas and statistical processes that have historically provided the best predictions of US elections. And there are definitely some methods that work better than the ones most of us see. But I won't; the answer for the problem with polls is not simply more accuracy—especially horse-race accuracy—from the pollsters and election forecasters.

Instead, the solution is two-pronged. First, the pollsters must update their methods for the twenty-first century. This book explores promising methodological developments in the public opinion industry—there are some exciting new ways to make polls more scientific and accurate. But this will not be enough on its own. The press and public must also adopt a new way of engaging with polls. If I'm able to show readers how to embrace the margin of error; how to understand the uncertainty inherent in surveys, and grasp the limits of polling to determine whether a very close election will tip in one direction or another, and still appreciate the utility of polling for government accountability, this book will have done its job. Americans have been watching election polls scroll across their screen without context for far too long. I want to help you to change the channel, moving away from the idea of polls as predictors of elections, and reenvisioning them as uniquely valuable for democracy.

There are two major lessons to keep in mind: First, polls do not give us a surefire prediction for the way people feel about a candidate or an issue; they only tell us one potential outcome along a distribution of values where opinions could potentially fall. And second, polls are a tool not only for electoral handicapping, but also for a responsive government. When journalists cover polling data, or when interest groups and regular citizens send numbers to their leaders, and when we modify the polls and calibrate the way we talk about them, polls hand a megaphone to the voice of the people, causing it to reverberate through the halls of government. Although the media may use them otherwise, polls are a distillation of the general will first—and everything else second.

POWER TO THE PEOPLE

The novelist James Joyce described Irish art as a vision in the "cracked looking-glass of a servant." Polls, too, are similar to a cracked mirror. We peer into them to divine the public's opinion. They tell us what we think as a collective body politic, flaws and all. We cannot look away, as we have incorporated them into our modern democratic process and the way we talk about politics. We want crystal-clear views of ourselves and the future, but the mirror frequently offers up a distorted reflection of the American public. Methodological shortcomings are cracks that are hard—sometimes impossible—to overcome; errors of interpretation and public understanding are scratches and smudges that need to be polished or wiped away.

That is the starting point for thinking of polls as serving a critical function in our society. Polls are better prepared to express the will of the majority and emergent minority than any single person, newspaper, or politician. This book will tell you how the science of that expression was built, how it can lose itself, and how we should rethink the polls going forward. Political activists, neutral poll-watchers, election forecasters, and the pollsters themselves will all play a part creating a future where the full potential of polls is realized.

But before we get there, we must relearn most of what we know about the polls. An accurate narrative history of public opinion, political polling, and the industry's role in modern journalism and democratic government is key to unlocking their full potential.

Along the way, we're going to see how intellectuals built the theory behind the polls. The first chapters of this book explore how the 2,000-year-old history of government censuses, ancient Athenian democracy, Jean-Jacques Rousseau's social contract theory, and the founding of the United States as a republic all shape the way we think about polls in the present. We will see how polls arose out of the ashes of inaccurate "straw polls," such as the one that the *Literary Digest* promoted in the 1920s and '30s, evolved as a tool for market researchers to haul in truckloads of cash, and then became a tool for pollsters to take the "pulse of democracy." We will learn how politicians use polls in the White House and in Congress, turning them, effectively, into elected representatives in their own right.

In the middle chapters, we see how over the last two decades, the widespread use of the internet and incredible advances in computation and statistics have elevated the science of political polling far beyond George Gallup's original, somewhat ad hoc methods. Pollsters working for political campaigns, such as the army of nerds in the boiler room of Barack Obama's reelection headquarters in 2012, have also reshaped the way pollsters think about the population of people who don't answer their calls. This history teaches us what to expect from polls, how they work, and what they're made of.

Finally, I address the modern history of the polls and discuss a path forward for fixing them—and how we think of them. In diving into some of the high-profile misuses of surveys, including potentially fabricated data sold to the US State Department, we will learn to appreciate how susceptible the science of polling can be both to ordinary human error and to nefarious intervention. These misuses of data are exceptions to the rule, but even good pollsters sometimes miss the mark. Polls are only reliable if a pollster ensures that the people they talk to are representative of the population as a whole. And while polling averages can cancel out the noise of individual surveys, chapter 5 discusses, it cannot fix bias that affects all of the underlying polling data. We will learn how election forecasting models work, how they try to account for these biases, and why they often come up short.

None of these issues will be solved by more, "bigger" data, smarter algorithms, or luck. Crunching the numbers will only get us so far. The way forward for the polls comes both from a collective realization of their inherent uncertainties and an embrace of their promise for our contract with government—especially in the years between high-profile elections. After all, there is no other tool that can do what polls do. What the Swedish mathematician Andrejs Dunkels famously said of numbers can also be said of public opinion surveys: It's easy to lie with polls, but it's harder to tell the truth without them.

ON THE SURFACE, this is a book about how polls work—about the art and science of sampling people from a large population and asking them what they think; about the history of one of the most important democratic institutions in the United States, though few acknowledge it as such; about "big data" and the information revolution; and about the damage done to the polling industry by an overconfident and naïve press.

It is also a book about the promise of those polls, and an argument for why we need them; about imagining a better democracy where the voices of the people are taken into consideration at every step of the political process—not to dictate government policy but to advocate, authoritatively and bolstered by objective data, for the general will of the governed.

In writing this book, my goal is to tell the enthralling story of the public opinion poll: to investigate, explain, and demystify it. But my hope is that it will also serve as a course-corrective both for how the polls measure the people, and for how the people measure the polls. If we can give polls a chance, understanding the scientific process that generates them, fully internalizing their margins of error, and valuing their insights for democracy even when they err, we may reveal a truer reflection of our general will.

STRENGTH IN NUMBERS

1

DEMOCRACY AND THE PUBLIC WILL

A man may not be able to make a poem, but he can tell when a poem pleases him. He may not be able to make a house, but he can tell when the roof leaks. He may not be able to cook, but he can tell whether he likes what is prepared for him.

—ARISTOTLE, *POLITICS*, CIRCA 350 BCE

In election years, news junkies are inundated with pre-election polls. Who is up today? Who will win tomorrow? What do the prognosticators think? But in fact, most political polls are not election polls, but issue polls. They gather people's attitudes on political problems and policies. How do Americans feel about gun control? About tax increases? About military spending?

Pollsters field questions on every aspect of American life to help shape news coverage, public policy, and further representation of the majority in our government. They have long hoped that activists and organizations will use their tools to make the political process more representative, fulfilling the promise and purpose of self-government. As the Harvard political scientist Sidney Verba explained in 1995:

> Surveys produce just what democracy is supposed to produce—
> equal representation of all citizens. The sample survey is rigorously
> egalitarian; it is designed so that each citizen has an equal chance to
> participate and an equal voice when participating.[1]

Although pollsters' recent blunders have tarnished this romantic view of their industry, surveys are nevertheless too crucial to our modern interpretation of democracy to simply cast aside. The stakes are much higher than whether election forecasters can predict the results of a contest before the votes are counted.

Opponents of majority rule frequently explain that the United States "is a republic, not a democracy." They define a "democracy" to mean a country where the people participate directly in their government, and a "republic," one in which voters elect a smaller subset of people to do the job of governing on their behalf. But the reality is that governments do not exist along this binary. Republics are forms of democracies, as they let people participate in the process of self-government.

It is obvious, upon reading the writings of the founders of the United States, that many of the most important men favored both republican and democratic principles. Their writings show they believed in political and electoral systems that both furthered the rule of a rational majority and pushed against it when it got carried away. One of the more forceful endorsements of majoritarian popular sovereignty came from James Madison, the Virginia statesman and "father of the constitution." In Federalist No. 10, a 1787 pamphlet arguing in favor of adopting a strong national government, he wrote that the realization of popular opinion must be the end goal of the political process. "If a faction consists of less than a majority," Madison wrote, "relief is supplied by the republican principle, which enables the majority to defeat its sinister views by regular vote."

Madison maintained his commitment to rule by the majority even when he was engaged in bitter factional disputes. In a 1791 letter to the *National Gazette*—one of the United States' early partisan "newspapers" that were little more than mouthpieces for the parties—Madison wrote that "public opinion sets bounds to every government, and is the real sovereign in every free one."

> Whatever facilitates a general intercourse of sentiments, as good roads, domestic commerce, a free press, and particularly a circulation of newspapers through the entire body of the people, and Representatives going from, and returning among every part of them, is equivalent to a contraction of territorial limits, and is favorable to liberty, where these may be too extensive.[2]

Shortly before he died, Madison wrote in a letter that the "vital principle of republican government is the lex majoris partis, the will of the majority."[3] For his part, Thomas Jefferson agreed, writing: "Where the law of the majority ceases to be acknowledged, there government ends, the law of the strongest takes its place."[4]

By the early nineteenth century, a belief in the ground truth and wisdom of the public's opinions had grown much more popular in American political thought. The concept of public opinion had also taken on a definition much closer to our modern understanding. Tunis Wortman, a Democratic-Republican from New York, wrote in his *Treatise Concerning Political Enquiry* that public opinion was simply "an aggregation of individual sentiments" that combined the beliefs of multitudes of minds, all bringing different aspects of their lives and experiences to their evaluations of the issues. This would cause "worse" opinions to correct each other, and for those higher-valued attitudes to prevail over the chaff. In this way, public opinion became "the ultimate triumph of Truth."[5]

These ideas have reverberated in American political thought since. James Bryce, the British ambassador to the United States between 1907 and 1913, wrote with high-minded idealism (and a bit of naïveté) about a "Government by Public Opinion" in his book *The American Common-wealth*, a sweeping study of American government and society in the vein of Alexis de Tocqueville's *Democracy in America*. Bryce wrote:

> [Public] opinion has really been the chief and ultimate power in nearly all nations at nearly all times. I do not mean merely the opin-ions of the class to which the rulers belong. I mean the opinion, unspoken, unconscious, but not the less real and potent, of the masses of the people. Governments have always rested and, special cases apart, must rest, if not on the affection, then on the reverence or awe, if not on the active approval, then on the silent acquiescence, of the numerical majority.[6]

It is tempting to view Bryce's comments strictly as an endorsement of direct democratic government—the form in which the people themselves decide what policies they shall adopt instead of allowing elected repre-sentatives to do the work for them. Indeed, Bryce also wrote lofty praise for the directly representative town hall meetings of Massachusetts: "The town meeting was a simple and effective way of articulating public opin-ion, and the decisions made by the meeting kept close to the public will." But a modern interpretation of his language, complete with surveys and polls, might conclude that the "unspoken, unconscious" public opinion extends farther than the attitudes expressed in voting booths. Bryce's ultimate goal was that "the people feel their supremacy, and consciously treat their rulers as their agents, while the rulers obey a power which they admit to have made and to be able to unmake them—the popular will."

Like many white scholars of his time, Bryce ultimately failed to live up to his own principles of democratization by refusing to support mass enfranchisement for Black Americans, and repeating disgustingly racist ideas about them. In 1910, Bryce appended a new chapter on what was then called "the Negro problem" to the third edition of *Commonwealth*.

He explained how the de facto political subjugation of Black citizens was preferable to equality on the grounds that "the period between 1873 and the adoption of these new [state] constitutions, a period during which, first by violence and afterwards by various tricks and devices...was worse than is the present legal exclusion of the great majority of them. It was demoralizing to the whites; it exacerbated feeling between the races; and as the Negroes were gaining nothing in those years by their nominal right to the suffrage, they have lost little by its curtailment." Bryce also called the "negro race" "lazy" and "inefficient"; said an African American man "plies his shovel with less vigor than an Irishman, and he is not so steady as a Chinaman"; and that African Americans had "an unchecked liking for vagrancy, and the Negro vagrant is prone to crime." "The average Negro is a naturally thoughtless, lighthearted, kindly, easygoing being, whose interests in life are of the most elementary order, and whose vision is limited to the few miles around his house."[7]

In an editorial for *The North American Review* in 1891, Bryce was harsher and clearer in his disdain for the Black population and their enfranchisement. He explained that the English whites in North America must "deal" with the many enslaved Africans who remain "ignorant, uncultured, swayed by passion rather than by reason" and who "cannot but be a source of danger, as well as a reproach to Christian civilization." The "vast majority" of African Americans, Bryce wrote, "are confessedly unfit for the suffrage.... Children of ten would have been fitter for such an experiment." The solution, in his mind, was to require residents to meet a minimum educational qualification to vote. This would decrease the influence of "the majority of colored voters [who] are not capable voters, competent for the active functions of citizens," as well as "the swarms of ignorant immigrants from the most backward populations of Europe."[8]

It is clear that James Bryce does not deserve some of the praise scholars have heaped on him. But we can nevertheless update his writing about the sovereignty of (white, male) public opinion by expanding it to all the residents of a country. Every person of legal age deserves their representation both by elected officials and by the polls. By quantifying the public opinion, political polls enable democratically minded citizens to hold their leaders accountable to it. They give citizens a gauge with which they can prove their leaders to be in line, or out of step, with the prevailing winds of democracy. And while we take for granted today that the public should at least be consulted in the process of governing, it was not long ago that the people were not listened to at all.

To understand the polls, one must first fully grapple with the weight of a democratic theory of government. We must understand that both the concept and the significance of public opinion took root gradually, and their development continues to this day. Once we understand the power of the people, we can come to realize the power of the polls.

THE SUM OF THE PEOPLE

The story of public opinion polling starts far in the past, long before the founding of the United States, the European Enlightenment, and even antiquity. It begins with a simple arithmetic question: How many people live around me?

An accurate census of the population can be thought of as a prerequisite to representative government, the assessment of public opinion, and the polls themselves. Before governments cared what their citizens thought about various public policy minutiae (and knew how to measure it), they simply counted them up. But giving individuals the idea that they are part of a single collective whole is an inherently democratizing idea. In an arithmetic sum of many ones, all units are equal. Enumeration helped pave the way to democracy.

Today, democratic societies also turn to censuses to measure the number of people who live in each political jurisdiction and to assign legislators appropriately—a process known as "apportionment" in the context of the United States Congress. Counting forms the basis of the link between the public and its representatives. A story of the birth of public opinion polling, then, might be helped by a brief retelling of the history of censuses.

States—loosely defined—have been counting the people within their borders for thousands of years. Although humans around the globe had been counting other things—livestock and vegetables, mainly—for even longer, most histories of population-counting begin with the Sumerians, who inhabited a quasi-city-state in what is now southern Iraq between 4500 and 1900 BCE. At that time, according to economist Andrew Whitby, who has written an authoritative historical account of how censuses evolved, any real counting would have been little more than an impromptu tallying of the number of people who lived in a particular area. Still, this would have been a novel development. Although it is unclear what counts of people were used for, they may have helped workers distribute food to residents or divvy up agricultural labors.[9]

Other examples of early censuses are much more recent. The Incas, who inhabited the Andes Mountains region of South America around 1430–1570 CE, are often theorized to have recorded population counts on strings tied in knots called *khipu*. Writing a few hundred years after the Spanish conquistador Francisco Pizarro wiped them out, Martín de Murúa recorded:

> They sent every five years *quipucamayos* [khipu-keepers], who are accountants and overseers, whom they call *tucuyricuc*. These came to the provinces as governors and visitors, each one to the province for which he was responsible and, upon arriving at the town he had all the people brought together, from the decrepit old people to the newborn nursing babies, in a field outside town, or within the town, if there was a plaza large enough to accommodate all of them; the *tucuyricuc* organized them into ten rows ["streets"] for the men and another ten for the women. They were seated by ages, and in this way they proceeded.[10]

China also has an ancient oral history of censuses enabling mass mobilizations and utilization of people. Whitby writes of a mythological emperor named Yu the Great, who placed the count of his people around 2100 BCE at exactly 13,553,923. That number is "almost certainly an embellishment," according to Whitby, who pegs it closer to 4 or 5 million at most. Either way, it is hard to know exactly what Emperor Yu would have used the figure for, as the record at the time is little more than myth.

Censuses became a core (and verifiable) function of the Chinese state around 700–300 BCE. Whitby credits this to Confucianism, which "emphasized good government, peace, prosperity, virtue, and justice, principles that were given force by a hierarchical bureaucracy and elaborate record keeping."[11] Confucian philosophy theorizes that good government would be rewarded with citizens through migration, according to Whitby, so enumeration became a test of whether Confucians were achieving such a goal. The philosopher Xu Gan wrote around 200 CE that the census could be used for purposes of taxation and conscription, as well as "apportioning land for fields and dwelling areas" and raising of people for hunting and other labors.

If the early Chinese really did count each other in order to distribute communal goods and services—only oral histories and secondary sources suggest they did—that would be an important milestone in the histories of both censuses and citizenship.

While inhabitants in the Far East were counting heads, so were those in the ancient Mediterranean and Middle East. Readers familiar with Judeo-Christian narratives will no doubt be aware of counting in classical times. Mary and Joseph are said to have given birth to Jesus Christ after traveling to Jerusalem for purposes of the Roman census, after all. But counting in the Near East began long before Jesus had arrived on the scene.

The first clear biblical reference to a census is in the Book of Numbers. God is said to have commanded Moses:

Take ye the sum of all the congregation of the children of Israel, after their families, by the house of their fathers, with the number of their names, every male by their polls; From twenty years old and upward, all that are able to go forth to war in Israel: thou and Aaron shall number them by their armies. And with you there shall be a man of every tribe; every one head of the house of his fathers.

The Bible refers to several other counts, of varying believability, including estimations that the Israelites numbered in the several millions, which was certainly an exaggeration, according to Whitby. And the Bible recounts that a plague was sent by God to punish King David for conducting his own census for the purposes of raising an army. Such godly wrath served as a reminder of the danger of census-taking for the next five centuries.[12]

Censuses are mentioned thereafter in histories of Egypt and Greece, according to the ancient historian Herodotus. In the 500s BCE, the pharaoh Amasis II "laid it down as a law of the land that each Egyptian, every year, should make a declaration before the governor of his province as to how he derived his living."[13] The ensuing taxation of the Egyptian people transferred so large a sum to state coffers that the Greek lawmaker Solon adopted the concept in Athens. The infamous census by Demetrius of Phalereus in Attica—the peninsula on which Athens lies—that took place in 317 BCE counted 21,000 citizens. The number of *metics* (or foreigners without the rights of citizenship) was around 10,000, and there were 400,000 slaves.[14]

Correspondingly, it is in antiquity that the story of censuses meets both the advent of democratic government and the creation of political philosophy itself. The emergent popularity of censuses may have given rise, as Leo Tolstoy put it, to "a mirror into which, willy-nilly, the whole community, and each one of us, gaze."[15]

Modern censuses serve a similar purpose to the ancient counts, though they are much expanded now. The United States Census Bureau has hundreds of thousands of permanent employees, and sends out hundreds of thousands of part-time workers every ten years to conduct a complete count of the population. The data are used to allocate federal resources, numbering in the hundreds of billions of dollars per year, and to apportion representation. An accurate count of the population is a prerequisite to thinking of citizens democratically, as parts of a whole.

THE ATHENIAN CENTURIES

The inhabitants of classical Greece—Hellenes, as they called themselves—established the world's first democracies around the middle of the last century BCE. Although there were several forms of government in the region around that time, most modern grade-school histories of this period focus on the city-state of Athens, and for good reason. Athenians lived under what Christopher Blackwell, a scholar of Hellenic history, calls a "radically democratic form of government" beginning in 508 BCE and lasting through the latter half of the fourth century.[16]

Although the emergence of democracy in Athens was a gradual process, 508 BCE nevertheless saw a few dramatic events that gave birth to a system of self-government that endured for nearly 200 years. In that year, Cleisthenes, a member of a wealthy aristocratic family called the Alcmaeonidae, led lower-class Athenians in overthrowing a tyrant ruler named Isagoras who had attempted to control the city with soldiers from Sparta, a rival Greek city-state. For his reforms, many historians have bestowed on Cleisthenes the title "the father of democracy."

In the reformed Athenian state, land-owning adult males enjoyed the role of co-governing citizens for the first time in history. They constituted the "demos" (the people), which made up the *ekklesía* (assembly), a citizen assembly and the first institution of mass direct democracy that was tasked with setting government policies and debating other measures.[17]

To keep track of all these citizens, the state kept an "Assembly List" of qualified men and the area they were from. Such ledgers acted as the database for all other democratic institutions in Athens—thus incorporating a basic form of enumeration into the very historical foundation of democracy. It is worth noting that the Athenian form of self-government was an unequal and oppressive one for most people. Only land-owning adult men who could prove they weren't slaves were incorporated into the demos, and allowed to make political decisions.

Cleisthenes's constitution (which was not a single document, as in the modern American sense, but rather a loose collection of independent rules and laws) was radical beyond its embrace of direct democracy. Not only could any citizen speak on matters of government, but the state also collectively recognized that interests—or opinions—could vary depending on one's location. Citizens in the countryside would be in more need of farming infrastructure than those living in and around the city, who might want funds spent on various buildings or monuments. Such tensions had been the cause of great strife in Athens in the past, so Cleisthenes created the "boule," a council of 500 men that set the daily agenda of the assembly.[18]

Although the Athenian government was structured with the Assembly as its foundation, the Council was explicitly charged with pursuing a "common good"—what we might consider today a balance between the needs and desires of the average voter—of all citizens. It was formed in a rather complicated grouping of citizens from different areas at various levels; The demos was first broken up at the village level, as "demes" (the precise number of which varied over time), then grouped into ten tribes that had roughly equal shares of men from the cities, coasts, and countryside. Each tribe selected fifty councillors from their respective demes.[19]

This was a radical invention. Through reforms, the Greeks implemented a novel theoretical approach to how the state should incorporate the people. Previously, the only question that was asked was who should govern. But now, the question was whether all citizens should govern—who deserved the right of citizenship, whether they had the capacity to do so, and how often they should participate.

The Assembly and Council held the power to propose laws and decrees, which were weaker versions of laws that were passed only by a vote of the Assembly rather than through a prolonged drafting process from a committee of legislators. Decrees proposed by the Council had to be approved by the members of the demos who gathered for the day's votes—a notable tool of mass democratic control over rule-making. Then, there were the popular courts, which had nearly unlimited power over the other institutions and magistrates.

While there were "republican" offices in the Athenian system—in the sense that a smaller number of people were making decisions for the whole—there were so many offices, all chosen through a system of "elaborate randomization" rather than popular election, that every citizen had the power to shape policy in some way. That is what made it a democracy, rather than a republic or any of the forms of self-representation that would come later. In fact, according to Blackwell's account, the extent of popular sovereignty in Athens ran so deep that a majority of citizens could have been chosen to serve as the executive officer of the Council[20]—as close to a president of democratic Athens as ever existed.

This form of "radical democracy" persisted with varying success in Athens for nearly two centuries. But in 322 BCE, Macedonian conquerors limited the authority of the Assembly over Athenian affairs and changed the constitution to restrict citizenship to Athenians whose wealth amounted to at least 200 drachmas—a medium sum, not enough to entirely escape the pressures of working-class life. This marked the end of "universal" (adult, land-owning male) suffrage in Athens.

THE REPUBLICS

The Athenian experiment has inspired long-lasting debates in political theory, especially about how much weight should be put on the opinions of the common person.

Democracy gives rise to the first theoretical frameworks for integrating public opinion into government procedures. To understand the role of polls in our political system, it helps to understand these roots of the normative debates over the value of a "public opinion." Although the term does not appear until the eighteenth century, in France, classical philosophers were discussing the subject long before.

It would be an intellectual betrayal of the political-philosophical dialogue to proceed without first mentioning Plato, perhaps the most famous Athenian philosopher, whose repeated objection to the city's political system shapes many modern characterizations of majority rule as "rank democracy" or "mob rule." Plato, like other classical philosophers, did not write extensively about the role of the masses in a democracy, but what he did write about the subject is important enough to the development of political philosophy that it is worth a brief discussion.

Plato was a skeptic of pure democracy (as were many of America's founders), which he thought was too susceptible to power-seeking politicians and demagogues who would corrupt the democratic system and lead the state into tyranny.[21] In the *Republic*, his famous work recounting Socratic dialogues about the ideal government, Plato writes:

"Come then, tell me, dear friend, how tyranny arises. That it is an outgrowth of democracy is fairly plain." "Yes, plain." "Is it, then, in a sense, in the same way in which democracy arises out of oligarchy that tyranny arises from democracy?"

Plato is speaking about the potential folly of giving power to the people. To Plato, the way democracies devolve political power allows fast-talking, passionate, and skilled politicians to so efficiently persuade their fellow citizens of an action or belief that the collective wisdom of the citizenry is polluted. Under democracies, says Plato, the demos is not full of leaders but of followers. And that enables nefarious actors to hijack the system for their own personal benefit. "The fiercest part of [the oligarchic class]," writes Plato, "makes speeches and transacts business, and the remainder swarms and settles about the speaker's stand and keeps up a buzzing and tolerates no dissent." The result is an oligarchic tyranny over the masses.

Plato's solution was, of course, an ideal one—which necessarily made it unattainable in the world of politics (where no ideals are realized). For all his talk of the pitfalls of democracy, Plato still believed that select members of the demos could indeed be trusted to run the state so long as they were properly educated and conditioned. According to Plato, good political order and proper education could produce "good natures in the state, and sound natures in turn receiving an education of this sort develop into better men than their predecessors."[22] Presiding over the affairs of the state would be a caste of philosopher-rulers, trained since childhood to be the most artful and politically skilled citizens. There would be special precautions to avoid their corruption (such as preventing them from owning land), and they would pursue the happiness of all citizens, regardless of what they wanted—for the philosopher-rulers knew best.

In terms of the modern legacy of Plato's political philosophy, the highest test is whether the "good natures" of an ordered, educated citizenry could still provide proper directions for actual societies, with their lack of omni-rational philosopher-rulers. And could a group of people, elected and accountable to the masses, adequately run the functions of the state? The example of *republican democracy* in Rome—the government of which consisted of both indirectly elected and appointed aristocratic leaders—begins to answer such questions.

As was true for Plato in Athens, the Roman statesman Marcus Tullius Cicero (106–43 BCE) did not write primarily about political matters. He is most remembered for his work on oratory and rhetoric. But what little he did write on matters of the state constitutes a notable stop on our brief history of public opinion in political thought. A politician, philosopher, and gifted speaker who briefly held the most powerful position in the republic (one half of the Consul, a dual-executive similar to the

American president), Cicero wrote three books concerning the state: *The Republic*, *On Duties*, and *On Laws*.

After a period of internal political disputes around the time of Cicero's life, Roman thinkers were growing increasingly frustrated with the way its government reconciled differences between aristocrats and the masses. Rome's republican constitution gave men the power to elect governing magistrates via popular elections, but not every man got an equal voice. Consuls such as Cicero were, for example, elected by a majority vote of the Centuriate Assembly, a body consisting of 193 unequal groupings of citizens into voting blocks called "centuries." Winners were determined by majority vote of each group, not the people within them. The richest and most propertied men were spread throughout centuries that voted first, while the poorest were crowded in higher-density centuries that voted last. This meant not all centuries had the same voting power, since tallies were recorded after each bloc voted, so those that cast ballots first usually decided contests before later centuries could even have a say. But the Assembly still gave the Roman people sovereign power over their Consul. This made popularity with the average (aristocratic) Roman essential to politicians' success or failure.

In Cicero's writings about the pressures that the public's opinions placed on elected magistrates, most often he invoked the term *opinio* to refer to the "general opinion" (*opinio omnium*) or the "opinion of the Roman people" (*opinio populi Romani*) in speeches or letters to his compatriots.[23] But he also mentioned the influences of the masses explicitly in his book *On Duties*. He wrote that a Roman politician had to frequently monitor the public sentiment, as "the eyes of all are cast on him. They examine whatever he does, the very way in which he lives; he is, as it were, bathed in so brilliant a light that no single word or deed of his can be hidden."[24]

Cicero's interpretation is a lesser form of the "public opinion" as it is formulated today, and more akin to the constant gossiping evaluation of political celebrities: more the public's opinions than the general abstract concept of the will of the people. But it is a step in the right direction.

PLATO AND CICERO'S WRITINGS show that the most prominent thinkers of the classical era believed that the public was both sovereign and dangerous. The Roman people, or *populus*, could give life to a magistrate's career as easily as they could take it away. Roman politicians would frequently face off against rumors and the whims of a people swept to action by powerful orators such as Cicero himself.

Advocates of democratization ought to credit Plato and Cicero as some of the first thinkers to formalize theories of how governments are accountable to their citizens. Yet they were simultaneously the first of note (along with Aristotle, Plato's famous student) to question the wisdom of that accountability. Both of these contributions would last well past antiquity; indeed, the debate rages on today.

THE "GENERAL WILL"

The concept of public opinion evolved slowly, if at all, in the 1,600 years following Cicero's death in 43 BCE—but then, like an earthquake, the idea erupted suddenly and with a bang. The Enlightenment brought with it the first widespread political theories that public opinion should formally operate as constant constraining force on government. Though at first it was but a crude philosophical concept, popular sovereignty took shape as a fundamental tenet of liberalism between 1600 and 1900.

Thomas Hobbes, an English philosopher who wrote most of his important works between the 1620s and 1650s, considered the public opinion to be a mechanical force, a product of citizens entering into a contract together to form an accountable government. In his most enduring work, *Leviathan* (1651), Hobbes wrote that government is "but an artificial man, though of greater stature and strength than the natural."[25] According to Hobbes, our collective public opinion is incorporated into the particular powers and arrangement of whatever government the participants might agree to form.

John Locke—whose writing inspired the Founding Fathers to include the phrase "life, liberty, and pursuit of happiness" in their Declaration of Independence—would go one step beyond Hobbes. Under his formulations of the ideal government, the masses would not only enter the governmental process at the point of foundation but also in an ongoing referendum on their actions. Speculating on the government's continual accountability to a sovereign people (and, later, on their fundamental right to revolution—which would also appear in Thomas Jefferson's contribution to the Declaration), Locke wrote that

> all power given [to the legislature] with trust for the attaining an end, being limited by that end, whenever that end is manifestly neglected, or opposed, the trust must necessarily be forfeited, and the power devolve into the hands of those that gave it, who may place it anew where they shall think best for their safety and security.[26]

Although Locke does not explicitly mention the "public opinion," he does write of a "political power" existing primarily for the ends of the "public good" of the society. In this way, Locke's *Second Treatise of Civil Government* (1689) was a big historical step toward seeing the government as a community endeavor with the "will of the people" as a guiding force.

No Enlightenment thinker did more to further the role that public opinion would play in emerging democracies than Jean-Jacques Rousseau. A Genevan who spent most of his life in France (often with warrants for his arrest), Rousseau is today celebrated for his manifesto on states, liberty, and representative government titled *The Social Contract*, which he published in 1762 at the age of fifty.

Before then, he studied both science and the arts (writings on which won him various prizes), and worked alongside other famous philosophers such as Denis Diderot. He also wrote a memorable autobiographical work called *The Confessions*, which was motivated in large part by the reputational blows he was dealt in his middle years. After a falling out, for example, Diderot called Rousseau "false, vain as Satan, ungrateful, cruel, hypocritical, and wicked. . . . He sucked ideas from me, used them himself, and then affected to despise me."[27]

When he was not fighting with his contemporaries, Rousseau was trying to answer Thomas Hobbes's big question: How do we balance the liberty of individualism with the authority of the state? Or, as Rousseau put it: How can the state be arranged such that its subjects find "a form of association which will defend the person and goods of each member with the collective force of all, and under which each individual, while uniting himself with others, obeys no one but himself, and remains as free as before"?

Rousseau envisioned the "general will" of all classes of people becoming the core mission of the state, and proposed that all institutions be structured around that goal. The means to that end is to make all governmental magistrates—in modern terms, elected officials—fundamentally accountable to the people, which he refers to as the "sovereign." This is a republican form of government. In a vein reminiscent of Locke's writing, the Rousseauian republic is one in which voters confer power on leaders, and retain their right to recall those leaders or enter into a new contract.

Of the several other constraining "relations" between citizens and the state that Rousseau wrote about, only one is germane to the purposes of this book. That final "relation" is the "public opinion; a power unknown to political thinkers, on which none the less success in everything else depends."[28] Rousseau considered this to be the "most important of all" and "graven . . . on the hearts of the citizens." He argued that it formed the "real constitution of the State" and "keeps a people in the ways in which it was meant to go."

This is the initial abstract construction of a "public opinion" that we have been waiting centuries for. Under Rousseau's formulation, the government is bound not only to the fundamental sovereignty of its participants, their individual voting decisions, and their collective needs but also to an elusive, ephemeral, and constantly evolving aggregation of their public-minded attitudes. In a republican government, if *l'opinion publique* is a true representation of the collective wisdom of the citizens, it must be given constant and immediate consultation in the processes of lawmaking and governing. Rousseau's social contract marks the punctuation between old-world political ideas and those that would flourish in the Americas, Europe, and the rest of the world over the next two centuries.

Still, the cumulative contributions of Rousseau and his predecessors leave two primary questions unanswered. First, how exactly should the public's opinions be incorporated into politics? And second, to what extent might individual interests, deficits of education, or other presumed shortcomings corrupt the general will? The debates over these questions have raged on, shaping discourse on democracy from the eighteenth century to the present.

HOW WISE ARE THE CROWDS?

Although the Founding Fathers of the United States integrated much of Jean-Jacques Rousseau's "general will" into their own writings, Platonian skepticism of the masses was still prevalent among the elite ruling class—and it shaped the government they created. Nearly all of the founders had a narrow definition of who counted as citizens—the most obvious violations of the universal right to representation being the widespread enslavement of Black Americans and the disenfranchisement of women. But James Madison also thought less of uneducated citizens, writing in a letter to Benjamin Rush, a supporter of the Constitution and onetime surgeon general of the Continental Army, that "if we are to take for the criterion of truth the majority of suffrages, they ought to be gathered from those philosophical and patriotic citizens who cultivate their reason, apart from the scenes which distract its operations, and expose it to the influence of the passions."[29] Jefferson maintained that the solution was not to disenfranchise less worthy white citizens but to educate them. He evidently considered Black Americans and women to be unworthy on different grounds.

Disagreement over the true "wisdom of the crowds," then, is an old tradition in American political thought. James Bryce was among the biggest champions of the public opinion, but he discriminated against many groups and otherwise faced much resistance. Alexis de Tocqueville, another European who came to the United States to study democracy in the 1800s, wrote in his 1831 book *Democracy in America* that public opinion was in danger of presenting an all-powerful "tyranny of the majority" over unpopular minorities and marginalized Americans. And, of course, many Americans were disenfranchised throughout history. Working-class white people, Black Americans, women, and Native Americans have all been regarded at some point or another as less capable of making the "right" decisions necessary for "good" self-government.

Pollsters today are often confronted by the similar criticisms of Walter Lippmann, a journalist and commentator most famous for his early-twentieth-century denouncement of "the mystical fallacy of democracy."[30] The philosopher John Dewey called Lippmann's 1922 book *Public Opinion* "the most effective indictment of democracy as currently conceived." Lippmann followed *Public Opinion* with another book titled *The Phantom Public*, in which he made the argument that the average citizen could never know enough to choose the right course of action. He used himself as an example:

> My sympathies are with [the citizen], for I believe that he has been saddled with an impossible task and that he is asked to practice an unattainable ideal. I find it so myself for, although public business is my main interest and I give most of my time to watching it, I cannot find time to do what is expected of me in the theory of democracy; that is, to know what is going on and to have an opinion worth expressing on every question which confronts a self-governing community.[31]

To Lippmann, "the world outside" is different from "the pictures in our heads" (phrases used in the title of the first chapter of *Public Opinion*), a poetic way of saying that our perceptions of the world are filtered by whatever biases we hold (or whichever blue or red partisan lenses cover our eyes, to further the metaphor). Chiefly because of the imperfections in the news media and our own psychological heuristics and stereotypes, he asserts, citizens can never deploy fully rational judgments on all the things that champions of true Athenian democracy would have to concern themselves with.

It is hard to disagree with Lippmann on these narrow arguments—or with the many Platonians who made them long ago. The size and scope of the government has ballooned since 1787, preventing any one person from being an expert in it all. And particularly in the twenty-first century, the media ecosystem has become so fractured and siloed that Americans are more likely to receive confirmation for beliefs they already hold (confirmation bias) than they are to experience new information that might make them think more critically, arriving at whatever "optimal" position exists for any given issue.

By way of empirical results, political scientists Scott Keeter and Michael Delli-Carpini devoted an entire book to this topic, *What Americans Know about Politics and Why It Matters*. They found eyebrow-raisingly low levels of knowledge of domestic politics among the masses. For example, less than a third knew what affirmative action was, and "more than 60% of [over 300 questions] could not be answered by as many as half of [people] asked."[32]

Elaborating upon Lippmann's skepticism of the people to make purely rational decisions, the political scientists Christopher Achen and Larry Bartels argue in their 2016 book *Democracy for Realists: Why Elections Do Not Produce Responsive Government* that voters do not in fact act rationally in accordance with the "folk theory" of democracy.[33] Instead, elections are fights between different factions of citizens in which our psychology is swayed by our affiliations to different candidates. Big-money special interests and identity politics also pervert rationalism, according to their "group-based" theory of democracy, and influence who gets to sit in the seat of power. In our modern democracy, the authors suggest, people don't think about which policies they want, but choose the political party that represents their culture and community and then adopt the orthodoxy of their fellow party members. If the general will is the cumulative opinion of polarized partisans and a "bewildered herd," can we really trust its wisdom?

THE MIRACLE OF AGGREGATION

You are probably skeptical of a "rule by the people" by now. But democracy's champions have cumulatively fashioned a compelling rebuttal to its critics.

We are first reminded of James Madison's emphasis that the "public opinion sets bounds to every government." John Dewey, also a critic of public opinion but who simultaneously believed the people were capable of attaining some degree of an "intelligent political life," made this case best in writing that "No government by experts in which the masses do not have the chance to inform the experts as to their needs can be anything but an oligarchy managed in the interests of the few."[34] To Dewey, public opinion serves as a guiding force for the government. One role for the polls is to let them set much of the agenda of government. Surely the people, together, can point out the things that are wrong; a good government would handle the rest.

Second, the singular "public opinion" masks a diverse multitude of publics, each exerting influence over other publics and potentially increasing the rationality of the average American. Political scientists have identified pockets of voters who are well informed on one issue or another, and might meet even Lippmann's knowledge-based criteria for adequately steering the ship of state on those issues. Most famously, Philip Converse, in his pathbreaking work in voter psychology and survey research, wrote of "issue publics" that offer specialized public opinion to government leaders. These are groups of voters "whose attentions center more or less continuously on specific governmental agencies or fields of policy"—and, crucially, who engage their political leaders and the media over these issues, thereby exerting force over both the government and broader public opinion. If voters work this way, not everyone needs to be offering "good" information to the pollster; rather, we just need to consult those who are paying the most attention.[35]

But what consequences could issue publics have on the broader will of the majority? We turn now to the phenomenon of "aggregation." The Greek philosopher Aristotle was much more sympathetic than his teacher Plato to the idea that the public was capable of making rational decisions. He admitted people could be irrational on many things on their own, but theorized that people were capable of wisdom when they respond collectively. It is worth quoting him at length:

> It is possible that the many, no one of whom taken singly is a good man, may yet taken all together be better than the few, not individually but collectively, in the same way that a feast to which all contribute is better than one given at one man's expense. For where there are many people, each has some share of goodness and intelligence, and when these are brought together, they become as it were one multiple man with many pairs of feet and hands and many minds.... And it is this assembling in one what was before separate that gives the good man his superiority over an individual man from the masses.[36]

Plato often referred to the masses as a "crowd" that was pushed and pulled by the loudest leaders within it. Aristotle's preferred "collective" and "public interest" is a distinct concept in the evolution of political theory. The idea of mass governance taking place in an impromptu meeting of citizens evokes a harsh image of a crowd of angry people trying a person and deciding to hang them in a public square. (Or, perhaps, of murdering them with hemlock, as Athenians did with Socrates.) But the term "public," as Aristotle intended it and as we understand it today, implied a more unifying people that are bound together by common interest. Their individual decisions are thus made for the betterment of the group. The crowd hangs a man for stealing bread from a neighbor; the public takes up a collection to buy food for people who have fallen on hard times.

Aristotle believed that, in aggregate, people could be wise. Certainly, the aggregate was wiser than any one randomly selected individual. Wisdom stemmed from the collection of individual "goods" into a whole, which canceled out randomly distributed "bads." This theory—which political scientists have come to call the "miracle of aggregation"—presumes certain conditions by which people come to their decisions. The idea that individual rationality points predominantly in a "good" direction while irrationality is randomly distributed is not at all obviously true. Given the influence of state propaganda, nefarious leaders, and biases in the aggregation process (through elections, where not everyone's voices are heard, or through self-interested representatives), this so-called miracle is no panacea.

Still, democracies are built on the theory that the collective is more rational than the individual. There is some evidence for this wisdom of people in aggregate. For example, the public opinion has generally been a leading indicator of where the government should move on questions of rights for marginalized groups, including on expanding voting rights for Black people in the 1960s and on allowing same-sex couples to wed throughout the 2000s and 2010s. People have tended to favor social safety nets, such as Medicare and Social Security, and spending on public works programs, like those of the New Deal, both of which improve the general quality of life for the average American. They are usually on the side of defending individual and minority political rights, especially for the First Amendment freedoms of speech, religion, and assembly. And after prolonged wars that produce many casualties, the public tends to revoke its support for intervention.

However, it is hard to conduct a study to quantify the rationality of people in aggregate. It would need to be done on the scale of a whole electorate, with proper definitions for the correct decisions on all issues, and the distribution of required information to a sample population of voters. But we can draw insight from animal sciences. One study conducted by a group of scientists led by evolutionary biologist Iain Couzin found that schools of fish can exhibit "democratic consensus" when they are searching for food. The team of researchers split one species of fish into two groups: one that was trained to swim toward a blue dot for a food reward, and another that was trained to follow their evolutionary instinct toward a yellow. When the two groups were placed together, with more blue fish than yellow fish, the minority's stronger "opinion" dominated the group's overall behavior, and the combined school swam toward the yellow dot. But when the researchers added fish with no bias toward either color, the fish increasingly swam toward the majority-preferred blue target.

Couzin and his coauthors used mathematical models to argue that we can expect similar findings among other species, including humans. "Conflicting interests among group members are common when making collective decisions, yet failure to achieve consensus can be costly," they write. "Under these circumstances individuals may be susceptible to manipulation by a strongly opinionated, or extremist, minority . . . but the presence of uninformed individuals spontaneously inhibits this process, returning control to the numerical majority."[37]

Under this theory, an ideal process of determining opinions would be more deliberative than survey-taking is today. You first have a pollster assess the positions of the public on an issue. You then have the press disseminate the will of the majority to the people. After allowing some time for community leaders to foster debate about the issue on which the people have received this information, you take a final poll to arrive at an informed measure of opinion on the issue. Although people are certainly more complex than the subjects Couzin studied, perhaps we can learn something from the fish.

Modern political science suggests that the rationality of the American public in aggregate is strikingly robust. In *The Rational Public*, a

1992 book on trends in polling throughout the twentieth century, political scientists Benjamin Page and Robert Shapiro meticulously trace the contours of the public's attitudes to key issues. Their work supports Aristotle's theory that the public opinion is wiser in aggregate than the average individual, who can fall prey to a lack of information and make an irrational decision about a policy that could benefit them. "Americans' collective policy preferences are real, knowable, differentiable, patterned, and coherent," the authors write. They are "generally stable; they change in understandable, predictable ways."[38] Page and Shapiro also assert a reasonably good match between real problems in the government and the issues that people rate as most important to them.

In their conclusion, the authors write that the public is "considerably more capable than the critics of majoritarian democracy would have us believe . . . the classic justifications for ignoring public opinion do not hold up." Their work is an empirical, full-throated counter to Lippmann's theorizing—though to be fair, the man did not have such data available to him seventy years earlier.

THE COURT OF PUBLIC OPINION

Finally, it is worth noting that, to V. O. Key and others, skepticism of the public often amounts to little more than destroying a straw man. In *Public Opinion and American Democracy*, perhaps his most heralded book, Key argues that the anti-democratic arguments deployed against public opinion—such as Walter Lippmann's—demolish only an "illusion" of the role that the public opinion plays in a democracy. His simplest criterion of representative government is that the public is getting roughly what it wants most of the time. In commentary reminiscent of John Dewey's, Key writes, "Unless mass views have some place in the shaping of policy, all the talk about democracy is nonsense."[39] Similarly, the political scientist E. E. Schattschneider once said that "we become cynical about democracy because the public does not act in the way the simplistic definition of democracy says that it should act. . . . The trouble is that we have defined democracy in such a way that we are in danger of putting ourselves out of business."⁴⁰

Political scientists such as Key and Schattschneider argued that public opinion serves a constraining role on leaders' choices, rather than a directive one. Rather than proposing a solution to a problem, polling data might simply restrict leaders to enacting a set of policies that are not dramatically unpopular. This is another of Key's proposals, proven later by Christopher Wlezien, who has studied the concept of the public acting as a "thermostatic" control of government. For example, when spending on a defense policy increases or decreases too much, Wlezien finds the public reacts by changing their preferences to bring policy back toward the middle. They have a vague sense of what they want—moderate spending— and hard preferences against anything that sways too far.

The English philosopher Jeremy Bentham (1748–1832) characterized the public similarly, but he went so far as to imply that popular attitudes constituted a separate institution of representative democracy. Bentham's "Public Opinion Tribunal" would, like a jury, punish elected officials if they strayed too far from popular actions. Penalties would take the form of a "moral sanction"—a public expression of the shame felt toward the errant leader. In Bentham's words, the Public Opinion Tribunal was "the only force . . . [by] which . . . government when operating in a sinister direction can experience any the least impediment to its course."⁴¹ Nearly two centuries later, the political scientist Samuel Kernell observed that President Bill Clinton was so ashamed of his falling poll numbers in the wake of the Monica Lewinsky scandal that he held a press conference to apologize for his adultery. The move won him a 17-percentage-point boost in his approval ratings.⁴²

One notable weakness of Bentham's Tribunal is that it assumes the public has quality information about politics and morality. Citizens would presumably receive information from the press and educational institutions. But not all newspapers provide accurate information, and not everyone receives a good education. Still, the burden placed on individuals by the Public Opinion Tribunal is much lighter than the spine-breaking load of policy knowledge and rationality that Lippmann required of the public.

THERE REMAINS ONE IMPORTANT REBUTTAL of these various critiques of democracy and the public opinion. If Americans are too naïve, uninformed, and polarized to participate rationally in politics—as Lippmann, Bartels, Achen, and others claim—that can hardly be their own fault. The day-to-day goings-on of middle- and working-class life afford little time for reading about the minutiae of government, and many of our attitudes are shaped by the information we receive from the media or government, which may be incomplete or inaccurate. People could have more time for politics if the government invested in more public works programs, created well-paying jobs for low-income families, or invested more in state and local economies. Poverty and a lack of education can make rational cognition difficult; both are, in part, failures of government policy.

The government is also at least partly to blame for the ills resulting from poorly regulated corporate television networks and social media websites that present readers with more fictions than facts. If monied special interests are contaminating our politics by funding interest groups, television advertisements, and news outlets that push their agenda, that is also something that our leaders can change.

Although pro-democracy theorists often avoid grappling with the potential contamination of public opinion by propaganda, that too would be the fault of the government, not of the people. A free press and the exchange of information over the internet provide two important checks against such contamination.

IN THE AGGREGATE, the public seems to know enough to make the right decisions on average. And they can control the excesses of government through the republican process. Informational shortcuts allow the less informed to approximate reason, and pockets of informed activism exert positive pressure over the whole. Plus, there are things other than attitudes on policy preferences that are extremely important for politicians to know: gut feelings about the world, general evaluations of quality of life, a prioritization of relevant policies, and approval ratings for government leaders are all taken into account in one way or another when deciding which issues to tackle and how to tackle them.

Americans are neither the whimsical mob that Plato and Lippmann feared, nor the "omnicompetent,"[43] rational citizenry that some pollsters and theorists would like them to be. The better philosophy lies someplace between the extremes of past theories. It offers a method by which the will of the people is incorporated into the process of governing, and therefore makes the outputs of government align more closely with the desires of the governed.

2

POLLING COMES OF AGE

Scientific polling makes it possible within two or three
days at moderate expense for the entire nation to work
hand in hand with its legislative representatives, on laws
which affect our daily lives. Here is the long-sought key to
"Government by the people."

—ARCHIBALD CROSSLEY,
"STRAW POLLS IN 1936," 1937

The earliest competitive US presidential elections were marred by
elitism, backroom deals, partisan mudslinging, and factionalism.
Partisan dominance by the Federalist Party in the last decades of
the 1700s and by the Democratic-Republicans through the early 1800s
caused presidential elections to be mostly uncompetitive. Only the predicted outcome of the 1800 election was really in doubt.

By 1824, new factional divisions had emerged. Although all the candidates for the presidency ran under the Democratic-Republican banner,
this fact only hid the competitive nature of intra-party squabbling that

had followed James Monroe's reelection in 1820. Various meetings of primary electors across the states selected Andrew Jackson, Henry Clay, John Quincy Adams, and William Harris Crawford for the final contest in November 1824. With so many candidates, none won a majority of Electoral College votes, and the House of Representatives decided on Adams even though Jackson had won the popular vote. (Jackson would use this infraction to launch his successful populist challenge of Adams in 1828.)

The competitiveness of the 1824 election paralleled an increase in the enfranchisement of working-class men. These changes spurred intense interest in the possible outcomes of the election. Given our innate desire to divine the future—and our devotion to anyone who we think can do so for us—people clung to any information that could offer clues as to the winner. In Pennsylvania, for example, observers kept records of the number of toasts made to the candidates at neighborhood Fourth of July celebrations. The tallies were repeated by the press as benchmarks that measured the success of each man's campaign.[1]

But perhaps the most reliable indicator came from a new record of vote intentions published by newspapers. The 1824 election marks the first recorded occasion of "straw polls"—the precursor to modern, scientific pre-election polling.

THE FIRST STRAW POLLS

Straw polls were informal, unscientific surveys of voter preferences, and they came in many different mediums with varying levels of sophistication. Among the most common were counts made at meetings of militia men.

Every year, county militias would hold "musters," where qualified men (usually those between the ages of 18 and 45) gathered in uniform to inspect arms and parade around town. In 1824, some musters were even called for the explicit purpose of assessing vote preferences. Upon meeting, someone would tally up mock votes for each candidate, and a newspaper would publish the results. For example, the *Carolina Observer* published this account of a presidential roll call vote on August 5, 1824:[2]

> At a company muster held at Maj. Wm. Watfard's, Bertie County, on the 17th July, in the afternoon it was proposed to take the sentiments of the company on the Presidential question, when the vote stood as follows:
>
> Jackson 102
> Crawford 30
> Adams 1
> Clay 0

In addition to straw polls of Fourth of July celebrants and militia members, spontaneous counts were taken at meetings of grand juries, tax gatherings, or any place where a group gathered that was interested in the upcoming election. Straw polls were also taken at rallies held on a candidate's behalf and at elections for other offices, where, for example, citizens would mark their preference for a candidate in a local election on one side of the ballot and write the name of a presidential candidate on the other. Given an array of such sources, newspaper editors would compile reports in cumulative tallies, updating the "poll" for readers each week.[3]

Although useful for generating news headlines and gathering attention for the press (much like modern polling), the earliest straw polls were not scientific and were subject to huge biases. A poll of militia men, for example, would obviously overstate support for Jackson, a general who fought in the War of 1812. And although some reports made an effort to obtain "a fair representation" of voters, newspapers reported on many other counts that were clearly not so evenhanded. Yet nineteenth-century newspaper editors, much like twenty-first-century "data journalists," found value in straw polls as a more desirable alternative to qualitative approaches, which mostly relied on endorsements and the opinions of local officials to gauge the status of the horse race. So published the *Observer* on July 29, 1824:

> The expression in black and white of numbers that are in accordance with facts rather than conjecture, is better evidence as to the popularity of men than whole columns of declamation, it is also better suited to the taste of the editor, who has a strong propensity to be what is significantly termed, one of the matter of fact men.[4]

The editorial bent toward hard data was, of course, inconsistent and often ideologically motivated. But it was an indicator of a larger shift toward numeracy and quantification in the nineteenth century. As historian Patricia Cline Cohen has noted, Americans increasingly came to believe that "mere opinion . . . would wither on the vine when challenged by the superior force of exact data. . . . In the nineteenth century, what counted was what counted."[5] Such a belief dovetailed with increasing democratization at the time, and supported the use of straw polls around the nation.[6]

HOW TO KILL A POLL

Straw polls began a dramatic change around the turn of the century. Many newspapers by then had noticed the weakness of relying on counts provided by military officers or everyday citizens and begun conducting their own straw polls. Among the earliest adopters of new straw-polling techniques were the *New York Herald*, *Boston Globe*, and *Columbus Dispatch*, as well as the *Farm Journal* and the *Pathfinder*, a weekly news magazine. As early as 1912, these publications mailed postcards soliciting opinions from their subscribers, or printed mock ballots directly in the issue and asked readers to cut them out, select their candidate, and mail the ballots back to the office to be counted by a team of reporters and editors.[7]

More sophisticated data-collection efforts were funded by the *Columbus Dispatch* and the *Cincinnati Enquirer*. They hired reporters to solicit mock votes in person, at hotels, offices, and on street corners. The *Dispatch* even adopted an early version of a statistical technique called "quota sampling," where canvassers were organized into separate crews so as not to duplicate work in the same part of the city, and were sent to cover both low- and high-income neighborhoods to ensure a diverse sample.[8]

Straw-polling expanded rapidly from there. In 1916, the *Herald* and *Globe* teamed up with the *Denver Republican* and the *Los Angeles Times* to conduct a poll of 36 states. By 1928, several newspapers owned by William Randolph Hearst were canvassing 46 of 48 states, and making predictions of the vote margins and Electoral College allocations in each. That year, newspapers conducted 85 straw polls of the presidential election (though most were conducted at the city or county level, rather than on a truly nationwide basis).[9]

Yet none of these straw polls ever reached the level of fame—or, perhaps, infamy—of the *Literary Digest* poll. In part, this was because none of them had the same reach. In 1924, the magazine mailed out over 16 million postcard ballots to owners of telephones and automobiles to test voter intentions in the presidential race.[10] The poll overestimated the share of the vote for Calvin Coolidge, the Republican candidate, in all but seven states. It overestimated the Republicans again in 1928, though it correctly identified the winner in every state except Massachusetts, Rhode Island, Alabama, and Arkansas.[11] However inaccurate, the *Digest* polls were slightly better than the average of other straw pollsters. But its consistent overestimation of Republican presidential candidates was caused by the upper-income bent of its sample, since it was drawn from lists of people who owned telephones or cars. These problems would later doom the *Digest* poll, and perhaps the magazine altogether.

In 1936, the *Digest*'s predictions of the presidential election were completely, utterly wrong. The magazine's final tally of returned ballots before the election gave Republican candidate Alf Landon 57% of the vote to

Franklin Roosevelt's 43%. But it was Roosevelt who would win, and by no small margin; The actual results on election night were 62% for Roosevelt and 38% for Landon (excluding third parties). The *Digest* had missed Roosevelt's vote margin by a whopping 38 percentage points.

Why did the *Digest* straw poll go so wrong? The root of the problem was twofold. First, as before, because the *Digest* sampling skewed upperclass, it had a built-in Republican bent. Archibald Crossley, the research director for the *Digest* for four years in the 1920s, speculated that this problem was worsened by the enthusiasm of Landon's supporters, who may have returned their ballots at higher rates than Roosevelt's voters. As Crossley's story goes, mail ballots are strongly influenced by feelings for candidates and are perfect avenues for casting "protest votes" against an incumbent president. But strictly speaking, Crossley was only speculating as to the psychological cause here. Social scientists had not yet developed the methods for peering into the human mind that they use today.[12]

Concrete evidence for this claim would only turn up a half-century later when, in 1988, a political scientist named Peverill Squire—then a newly minted PhD graduate from the University of California, Berkeley—re-analyzed polling data that asked voters about the *Digest* straw poll by a then-little-known pollster named George Gallup. Gallup had fielded surveys after the election and asked voters if they had received a "straw vote ballot" from the *Digest*, whether they sent it in, and who they voted for. He found that people who owned neither a car nor a phone—and would therefore be excluded from the *Digest* poll—supported Roosevelt by a margin of 60 percentage points, 79% to 19% for Landon, while those with both a car and a phone only gave Roosevelt a 10-point margin. Further, Squire found that the voters who decided to mail back their ballots were even more unrepresentative than the list itself. They favored Landon by three points, while those who didn't submit their straw votes went for Roosevelt by 39 points. Although these data do not fully reproduce the *Digest*'s ill-fated estimates, they provide hard evidence for Crossley's claims.[13]

After the election, the *Digest* ran a cover titled "Is Our Face Red!" It was criticized widely for its inaccurate prediction. The *New York Herald Tribune* even went so far as to denounce all polls, including George Gallup's (which it had spread across pages just days earlier and produced accurate predictions of the election results). The *New York Times* wrote, "The result on Tuesday has made [the *Literary Digest* poll] and most other polls of the kind only straws which the wind driveth away. American voters can well get along without its guidance or misguidance in the future.... Should it never appear again it will not be missed."[14]

Ashamed, the *Literary Digest* never published a straw poll again, and the magazine shut its doors two years later in 1938.

MAKING A POLLSTER

Not many people saw the *Literary Digest*'s failure coming. George Gallup was the most prominent of the few who did.

In 1936, Gallup was a balding, well-kept Midwestern ad man with a welcoming smile but an imposing presence. Born in 1901 to a farming family outside Jefferson, Iowa, he spent his time outside school milking the six cows on his family's farm and playing football and basketball. He was an unassuming young man who liked to work long hours in devotion to his craft—perhaps a product of a legacy of puritanism in his community, according to one biography. Under a photograph of his high school graduation in 1919, Gallup wrote, "Leave the women alone, work hard and enjoy life is my motto!"[15]

At the University of Iowa in Iowa City, Gallup grew enamored with journalism. He became an adept newspaperman, eventually heading up the student newspaper, *The Daily Iowan*, a position for which he assumed all costs and liabilities (as was the tradition of the university). Circulation was low, and while students previously had not wanted the financial risk associated with running a newspaper, Gallup spied an opportunity for a big reward. To attract the attention of the campus, he wrote an editorial in the summer of 1921 titled "The Unattractive Women," which chastised female students for being poorly dressed and having loose morals. It made the paper a must-read almost overnight. By 1923, the paper was a fully fledged urban daily newspaper, with Gallup as its chief editor. As the readership of the *Iowan* grew, so too did its advertising revenue. Upon earning his bachelor's degree in February 1923, Gallup remarked that his earnings from the paper (and some other odd jobs) totaled more in salary than that of the president of the university. He stayed at the university until he earned his PhD in 1928.[16]

What was Gallup's secret? Besides hard work and attention-grabbing headlines, he also reinvented the way that newspaper editors figured out which articles and columns were most read (and thereby generated the most ad revenue). He borrowed tactics he developed for other newspapers and applied them to the school paper. For example, during a 1923 summer job conducting a readership survey by the D'Arcy Advertising Agency in St. Louis, Gallup found that a high percentage of respondents claimed that they always read the editorials and news. But few admitted reading the gossip columns and other articles "of low prestige." He was suspicious of this, so he devised a more accurate way of measuring readership. He would place a fresh copy of the last issue of the newspaper in front of a person, then would follow as they went "column by column, page by page . . . to see what he or she had read in this particular issue." The survey findings brought to light an interesting fact. The newsiest articles published in the newspapers attracted far fewer readers than the typical questionnaire indicated. Conversely, the comic strips, the love advice features, and the like had considerably more readers.[17]

Drawing on his experience at D'Arcy, Gallup tested his new method in a formal experiment for his PhD dissertation at the University of Iowa's psychology department. He later published a version of his work in the magazine *Editor and Publisher* under the title "Guesswork Eliminated in New Method for Determining Reader Interest."

When Gallup later applied his novel method of audience measurement to the *Des Moines Register*, he found striking levels of inaccuracy in the *Register*'s measurement methods. It turned out that none of the respondents who claimed to read the whole paper ever read more than half; the front page, crammed with domestic and international news, was rarely read; and most reader attention was given to cartoons, comics, photographs, and obituaries—then considered to be secondary focuses of the paper.

Gallup's dissertation and corresponding consulting are notable not only for his ingenuity at newspaper marketing but also for being the first formal instances of Gallup surveying people to better understand their attitudes and behaviors. The act of sitting someone down to watch them read a newspaper would turn out to be remarkably similar to asking them how they felt about a war. Gallup's newspaper surveys can be understood as the first point on his path toward becoming the father of modern public opinion surveys.

THE SECOND STOP on George Gallup's journey was a profitable and decades-long foray into advertising and market research. After completing his PhD and while teaching psychology at the University of Iowa, Gallup was hired directly by Raymond Rubicam, founder and president of the prestigious New York–based advertising firm bearing his name, to run the firm's research department. Rubicam gave him free rein to do nearly anything he wanted. At Young & Rubicam (Y&R), he used survey methods to improve the readability and memorability of the agency's advertisements. Gallup's efforts worked; Y&R's revenue increased from $6 million in 1927 to $22 million a decade later.

Gallup's genius—as a journalist-turned-publisher and as a marketer—amounted to various applications of a very simple principle: ask the people what they want. At Y&R his major contribution was the development of a scoring system called "Impact," which quantified how well customers remembered advertisements. The theory was that ad memorability in, say, a grocery store would lead to higher sales for the associated brand. The score was based on telephone interviews in which Gallup's employees would ask respondents to recall ads that they had read, seen, or heard the day before. These first efforts to measure attitudes via telephone would shape the rest of his career, mainly by giving him confidence in his ability to obtain high-quality samples of opinions.

AMERICA SPEAKS

After fine-tuning his research methods, George Gallup turned his attention to public opinion and electoral polling. Although it's unclear exactly what motivated this shift, accounts propose several factors that perhaps built upon each other until he was finally pushed into polling about politics full-time.

According to some accounts, Gallup was intellectually unsatisfied by an otherwise profitable and prestigious career as a research executive at Y&R. In one interview he recalled, "By nature, I've always believed in change. I guess I've always had a messianic delusion." Indeed, one of Gallup's best-known college newspaper columns was titled "Be Radical!" He wrote, "Don't be afraid to be radical. . . . Doubt everything. Question everything. . . . Being a radical is a duty, like casting your first ballot or kissing your sister. Only a man of fifty has the right to be conservative. Don't be a cow. Think, question, doubt! Be radical!"

Gallup also appeared to have noticed a gaping hole in the market for political opinion research. Just as you could ask people which advertisement campaigns they liked better, you might also be able make a load of money asking them what types of politicians and policies they preferred. You could probably even sell that data to people who were interested in it. A 1948 profile of Gallup in *Time* magazine recounted him saying to himself, in 1932, "If it works for toothpaste, why not for politics?"[18]

If there was any single moment when Gallup's career as a political pollster was launched, it was in 1932. Back then, when straw polls were still all the rage, Gallup had his students in Iowa conduct "a few rather crude samples" to help his mother-in-law, Ola Babcock Miller, win election as Iowa's first female secretary of state.[19] His son, George Gallup Jr., later said that Gallup's success that year "certainly inspired him and empowered him to move forward with polling."

In 1935, while still at Young & Rubicam, Gallup founded the American Institute of Public Opinion—now Gallup, Inc.—in Princeton, New Jersey. He invested in the business himself, but also raised capital from the likes of Harold Anderson, who ran Publishers-Hall Syndicate, a newspaper syndicate out of Chicago. Anderson had a keen eye for what content could generate revenue, and polls were near the top of the list. That October, Anderson published Gallup's weekly newspaper column about his poll results, called "America Speaks," in over thirty newspapers across the country. When Gallup released the results of his first nationwide survey, a small airship cruised over Washington, DC, announcing the news.

GALLUP BECAME THE FACE of "scientific" public opinion polling in 1936, when he predicted (along with a few other "pollsters," as they were soon dubbed) that Franklin Roosevelt would win the election. He embraced the publicity that came with being at odds with the *Literary Digest*'s straw poll, seeing the tension both as a source of potential legitimacy for scientific opinion polling and an enormous money-making opportunity.

In fact, he was so confident in his new methods that he offered a money-back guarantee to any newspaper or magazine carrying his predictions, that he would be more accurate than the *Digest*.[20] This drew a quick and harsh reaction from the magazine's editor, Wilfred Funk, who wrote an open letter in the *New York Times* that "never before has anyone foretold what our poll was going to show before it was even started! . . . Our fine statistical friend [Gallup] should be advised that the *Digest* would carry on our poll with those old-fashioned methods that have produced correct forecasts one hundred percent of the time."

That decision turned out to cost the *Digest* everything, while making Gallup richer and more famous than any pollster before him—and any pollster since. In November, Gallup's poll showed nearly the opposite of the *Digest*'s, forecasting 56% for Roosevelt to Landon's 44%.

How was Gallup able to beat the best-known straw poll in the country? His most important innovation was to "sample" smaller numbers of poll respondents in a way that would make the whole of them more representative of the electorate, rather than sending a postcard out to every person on a list and hoping respondents reflected a portrait of Americans. Initially, Gallup's process for this was to send teams of workers around the country to interview voters in person, dividing respondents into different buckets by race, income, and geography so they would be reflected in the poll in proportion to their numbers in the actual population. If 90% of voters where white and 50% owned an automobile, Gallup's theory went, then his "quota-controlled" poll should roughly match those demographics. This gave him a clear edge over the *Digest*'s method, which (as we have seen) gathered answers from all respondents irrespective of their demographic characteristics, which led to severe biases in the polling. In 1936, with a widening class divide between voters for Landon and Roosevelt, the magazine failed to sample enough low-income voters. Gallup's polls did much better, a victory for him and for "scientific" polling.[21]

Gallup's high-profile victory is the beginning of our political and cultural obsession with pollsters, but his company was not the only innovator in the field of public opinion research. Gallup's contemporaries included many scientists of polling, including Elmo Roper (who started the Roper Center for Public Opinion Research at Williams College in Massachusetts), Archibald Crossley, Hadley Cantril, and Harry Field (who founded the National Opinion Research Center, an academic polling organization, at the University of Denver in 1941)—to name just a few.

But even among those who came after Gallup, none made quite so public an impact on the field. A 1944 survey[22] found that 56% of Americans had heard about public opinion research, with 60% of those recognizing the Gallup Institute (and only 7–11% recognizing Roper and Crossley). Today, Gallup's name is practically synonymous with polls—no other names are as widely recognized.

After the 1936 election, Gallup's company flourished. He founded polling agencies in Europe and expanded his domestic enterprise. "America Speaks" was soon carried in over 200 newspapers or periodicals. Gallup enjoyed more success than the *Digest* ever did. And he had scientific innovations in public polling to thank.

The next two presidential elections were relatively good ones for pollsters. They got the election "right" in both 1940 and 1944, and in the latter election, all five major pollsters—Gallup, Roper, Cantril, Crossley, and Field—got Roosevelt's share of the popular vote within two percentage points.[23] However, the pollsters soon learned that hot streaks rarely last forever.

DEWEY DEFEATS TRUMAN

Political pollsters and election forecasters often remark that their work is part art and part science. But it is also part luck—and if 1936 was a lucky break for George Gallup and the pollsters, 1948 was a dramatically unlucky one.

That year, the final polls from each firm indicated that Thomas Dewey, the Republican candidate, would defeat Harry Truman, the incumbent Democratic president, by anywhere between five and fifteen percentage points. The pollsters were so sure of Truman's defeat that they stopped polling altogether by mid-October. Elmo Roper called it quits even earlier, writing on September 9 in the *New York Herald Tribune* that the gap between the two candidates was too large for Truman to overcome. He reckoned that, because the previous elections had been rather uneventful, campaigns were "largely ritualistic," predictable, and cyclical affairs shaped by underlying structural factors far in advance of the outcome. "The evidence we have accumulated since 1936 tends to indicate,"

Roper wrote, "that the man in the lead at the beginning of the campaign is the man who is the winner at the end of it. . . . The winner, it appears, clinches his victory early in the race."[24]

The pollsters were not alone in putting it all on Dewey. Political bookmakers put the payout for Truman winning in the fall at 30 to 1—paying $30 to every $1 bet for him, coming out to a just-greater-than-3% chance he would come out ahead—and improved the odds only to 4 to 1 (a 20% chance) by Election Day. Many reporters also counted the president out; the *New York Times* predicted that Dewey would win 345 electoral votes, and the *Wall Street Journal* wrote that "government will remain big, active, and expensive under President Thomas E. Dewey." *Life* magazine ran a cover with a full-page photograph of Dewey, calling him "The Next President." Even Walter Lippmann, stalwart opponent of the polls, wrote about Dewey's inevitable victory and the foreign policy challenges he faced.[25] Virtually nobody thought that Truman stood a chance.

History determined these conclusions were all premature. In the final weeks of the election, Truman embarked on a whistle-stop tour of America that is widely credited for turning around his campaign. On November 2, 1948, he defied the polls and prognosticators and beat Thomas Dewey by five percentage points in the national popular vote. The then-unbelievable upset led to the famous photograph of Truman standing on the presidential train in St. Louis holding up a copy of the *Chicago Tribune*, which had gone to the printers before the election results were known, with the headline DEWEY DEFEATS TRUMAN.

The 1948 election was the most humbling defeat for scientific opinion polling yet. *Time* called it "The Great Fiasco," and the *Pittsburgh Post-Gazette* remarked that "we won't pay any attention any more to 'scientific' predictions and we don't think our readers will."[26] The *Detroit Free Press* ran with the headline TRUMAN: 304, POLLSTERS: 0—a reference to the president's large electoral vote tally.[27] Will Funk, formerly editor of the *Literary Digest*, was quoted in the *Washington Post* as having said, "I get a very good chuckle out of this . . . nothing malicious, mind you. We were told by contemporary pollsters [in 1936] that we had been unscientific. I'm afraid they made the same mistakes. I'm afraid the word 'science' isn't going to be used with a poll for a long time."[28] Funk's critique missed the mark in some ways, but it serves as a good reminder to pollsters that there are many reasons for humility in polling—"scientific" and otherwise. Cockiness is a pollster's kryptonite. Warren Mitofsky, the pioneering pollster who later developed random-digit dialing to obtain probability samples via the telephone, said of 1948 that pollsters "should not be too arrogant.... Every time you get cocky, you lose."[29]

Even at their best, polls cannot give us a perfect measure of what the public wants. That is inherent to their design. Public opinion polls are surveys of a subset of people chosen from a larger population of Americans. Traditionally, the members of those groups have been chosen to represent the overall population, based on the theory that randomly surveying a small selection of people can accurately paint a picture of what we all collectively think.

But there is always room for error in a poll. In any selection of 1,000 people from a group of over three hundred million, you are bound to survey some oddballs just by random chance. Or, again by random chance, you might miss the opinions of a key demographic and bias your poll against them.

This is why pollsters (the good ones, anyway) always release their estimates with a margin of error that alerts a poll-reader to the degree to which a finding could be incorrect, just given random variation in the individuals the pollsters talked to. If a poll came out tomorrow that said 20% of Americans hate Coca-Cola, but the data have a margin of error of five percent, we shouldn't be surprised if, after asking all 300 million of our compatriots, the true share of Coke-haters is as high as 25% or as low as 15%. Similarly, if a poll proclaims that candidate A leads candidate B by five percentage points, but with a five-point margin of error, we should understand that it does not mean the poll has called the election for candidate A. Read properly, the poll instead indicates that candidate

A should win *most of the time*, but candidate B will win in the rare circumstances where the pollsters got a bad batch of respondents.

But how "rare" are those misfires? According to the statistical theory, a pollster's margin of error represents their guess at what the poll could say if they repeated the procedure in exactly the same way twenty separate times. For example, a 3% margin of error tells us that in nineteen (or 95%) of those polls, the surveyors will get something within the 3% margin of error of the first poll. But in any given poll, according to the laws of statistics, the result could be outside the range of expectations. In this way pollsters' margins of error do not firmly rule out possibilities— rather, they take into account the roughness of the underlying data that make up a poll.

SCIENCE IS MAGIC THAT (SOMETIMES) WORKS

After the 1948 election, a group of researchers at the Social Science Research Council (SSRC) convened to arrive at a conclusion as to why the polls went so wrong. Gallup, Crossley, and Roper all cooperated with the committee, sharing their data and lending resources in other ways. A Harvard statistician and member of the council named Frederick Mostellar wrote that "an authoritative factual inquiry was needed to terminate the growing controversy or to focus discussion upon specific issues at the earliest possible moment."[30] It seemed that pollsters couldn't have agreed more.

The SSRC's conclusions were in part obvious, but also raised important methodological suggestions for future polls. First, they wrote that the failure "to detect shifts in voting intentions during the later stages of the campaign" and the assumption (pronounced most publicly by Roper) that "the voting intentions would not change during the campaign" were the biggest sources of potential error.[31] Indeed, with the benefit of hindsight, this was a clear miscalculation. Being composed of many academic social scientists, the council also suggested that the prediction of human behavior was a "hazardous venture" that would need to be improved upon by incorporating more research and knowledge from social psychology and political science into the polling process. Both of these recommendations remain starkly relevant over sixty years later.

The council also recommended that the pollsters make several methodological changes, writing that there were "better techniques now available, particularly in sampling and interviewing," than the ones pollsters were using.[32] They were right. The shoddy way many early polls were conducted might surprise readers today. Decisions about methodology or data analysis were often arbitrary, even seat-of-the-pants. For example, the pollsters would send teams of researchers to fan out in city streets to interview anyone who fit their demographic quotas. Researchers would keep track of their sample distribution, counting the numbers of Black respondents or women who needed to be added to the mix and would then hunt for the next respondent. The mental image of a man in a black three-piece suit and matching fedora standing by a lamppost pushing a clipboard upon passersby is not so far removed from the actual practices of many interviewers.

But by 1948, the survey research community acknowledged significant issues in polls conducted by such "quota sampling" methods, in which polls sampled the opinions of a certain number of people from various demographic groups (organized by age, sex, or income). Chiefly, they knew that they had a big problem with selecting respondents who weren't truly representative of the "public." One popular (perhaps apocryphal) anecdote showed the way such biases work. In it, an interviewer coming across construction workers eating lunch decides to knock five or ten interviews out in a short amount of time. The first interview might be an expression of the respondent's true feelings, but subsequent respondents would fall prey to peer pressure or other psychological forces. And a 1949 book by Morris Ernst and David Loth (a lawyer and civil servant, and a journalist, respectively) documents the story of a young part-time interviewer who, when short of time, would substitute interviews with farmers with interviews with his housemates, asking, "If you were a farmer, what would you answer?"[33]

Adam Berinsky, a political scientist and survey research expert, found that interviewers were more likely to walk around in neighborhoods where residents were better educated. Accordingly, George Gallup's polls had about three times as many college-educated voters as they should have had.[34] Interviewers were also reluctant to spend time in lower-income neighborhoods and in parts of town with more African Americans. One field interviewer for Elmo Roper's poll once wondered whether it was "safe or wise to work" in a "Negro section" of town. A person "might have run into serious trouble if they weren't able to cope with a situation quickly and tactfully," she wrote.[35] And even if she did proceed, the differences of skin color and class between the interviewer and respondent were bound to create unreliable answers.

These individual decisions tended to add up to samples that were whiter and more upper-class than they should have been. As a result, many political scientists dismiss the polls from the 1930s and '40s entirely. The professor of voting behavior Philip Converse later wrote that data in this era were "collected by methods long since viewed as shoddy and unrepresentative."[36]

The SSRC's proposed alternative to quota-controlled polls was a method called "probability sampling," where each person is assigned an equal probability of being chosen for an interview. This design was most theoretically satisfying to mathematicians and academic public opinion researchers, who argued that randomly selecting enough people from the population of voters is the only statistically sound way to make sure a poll is representative.[37]

However, despite the issues with quota sampling, pollsters had resisted calls for a switch to more truly scientific sampling methods. Archibald Crossley wrote that probability sampling was "very difficult to use right,"[38] as well as being slow and expensive. Since interviewers would have to conduct repeated phone calls or visits to households that did not respond to their initial requests, fielding periods were longer, which meant interviewers had to be paid for additional labor.

This resistance eventually proved to be futile. Academics' enthusiastic embrace of probability samples very quickly bled into the public polling industry. By 1950, Gallup had started converting certain segments of his methodology to the more theoretically sound design. Instead of going house to house and interviewing people if they met certain demographic characteristics, Gallup's researchers selected households randomly via a stratified, "nested" design. For a national poll, for example, pollsters would split the country up into different regional chunks. In each, they randomly selected a group of cities or "minor civil divisions" (sparse rural areas); then a random group of precincts within them; and finally, a random group of households in each chosen precinct.[39] The improvement in method helped fix a tendency for Gallup's polls to have too few Southern voters.[40]

The near-ubiquitous installation of landline telephones in American households in the following decades also aided the switch to probability sampling; it is easier to dial a new number or conduct a telephone callback than it is to repeatedly travel to a person's home to interview a specific respondent. By the late 1980s, upward of 98% of polls from major firms were conducted over the phone, and a majority had moved away from quota controls.[41]

The legacy of the 1948 fiasco was thus threefold. First and foremost, it humbled the pollsters by reminding them that the patterns of past elections were not guaranteed to persist into the future. The population of "undecided" voters who, a week before the election, had still not made up their minds and could sway the outcome of the contest at the last minute has been top of the mind for pollsters ever since.

Second, it led to a highly public reckoning with the methodological weaknesses in the early polls, and a corresponding shift to truly modern tools. After 1948, polls began to look much more like the "science" that George Gallup had promised all along, with statistically sound samples and a constant experimentation with new, better methods, and less like the art of guesswork that had failed the industry before. Accordingly, pre-election polls in the 1950s were much more accurate than those in the 1930s and 1940s.

Finally, the contest was the first lesson to the people that even "scientific" polls could err. This is a natural expectation of the process of sampling: even if they are truly picked at random, a group of 1,000 Americans is not going to perfectly represent a country as demographically and political heterogeneous as the United States. The people willfully responding to polls might be further unrepresentative of the overall population. But as recent elections have shown, consumers of polling data have still not fully internalized this troublesome fact.

OPINION'S CLOUDY PATH

The popularity of pollsters in political and academic circles in the late 1940s also brought about a renewal of the old battles over the place that public opinion has in the democratic process. The idea that the government should be responsive directly to the people was no longer a theoretical one, an impractical proposal that had garnered relatively little support among the men who designed the country's institutions. The widespread availability of polling caused a break with the dominant, elitist ideology that had shaped American institutions in the century and a half since the founding. By distributing the information about public opinion via popular newspapers and books, Gallup and his contemporaries fostered government responsiveness.

Gallup worked tirelessly throughout his career to elevate polling to be respected enough to impact the government. Gallup believed, in contrast with his critics—empirical and otherwise—that the opinions of "the common man" (today, "and woman") would reflect in aggregate the wisdom required to improve the positions of both the country and its inhabitants—something James Bryce had only dreamed of. In his 1888 book *The American Commonwealth*, Bryce had written, "The more completely a popular sovereignty prevails in a country, so much the more important is it that the organs of opinion should be adequate to its expression."[42] While no comprehensive tool for gauging "the organs of opinion" existed when Bryce wrote these words—and he may have excluded many voices if it had—Gallup's work paved a new path.

Bryce's theory became Gallup's driving motivation for popularizing political polling. Both have shaped the ideas that their many successors and students have iterated upon. In *The Pulse of Democracy: The Public-Opinion Poll and How It Works* (1940), Gallup and coauthor Saul Forbes Rae wrote about the polls serving as a constant referendum on the processes of our government:

> For the first time in democratic history, continuous surveys of what America thinks are enabling us to collect the facts about public opinion. Public-opinion research provides an objective week-to-week description of the values to which the people hold, and the prejudices and attitudes which they have formed out of their own experiences.... On the basis of "early returns" from the common people, the prediction may be made that government responsive to the average opinion of mankind will continue to survive long after dictatorial systems have become mere bogey stories to frighten our great-grandchildren.[43]

This ability to continually measure the "pulse of democracy" reignited old debates over how keenly politicians should listen to the people. At the crux of this debate was the question of whether politicians should be left to act upon their own opinions, or if they should follow public sentiment as revealed by the latest poll. Leaders versus followers—the politicians versus the pollsters.

Such criticism of polling was the point of the most scathing rebuke of the enterprise yet. Lindsay Rogers published *The Pollsters: Public Opinion, Politics and Democratic Leadership* in 1949 (it had mostly been written before the 1948 forecasting fiasco). Rogers was a political scientist at Columbia University between 1929 and 1959, a period that saw a massive shift of academic political science away from the old theory- and history-driven study of politics. New students and professors placed more focus on behavioral studies of how voters thought and acted, and most of these studies were driven by political polls. But Rogers was more of an institutional thinker, concerned with the contemporary and historical dynamics of government.

Rogers's background made him a sort of "old guard" in political science, a position made clear by the arguments he presents in *The Pollsters*. To Rogers, polling was not only methodologically flawed but a betrayal of American democratic theory. He maintained that our republican form of government incentivized independent leadership and deliberation by elected officials. And for all their shortcomings, he thought legislators were better able to perform the duties of government than the mass public was. "True it is," Rogers writes, "that representative bodies often yield to selfish pressures and sometimes enthrone privilege, but representation permits a greater measure of compromise between clashing opinions and interests than when decisions are made by the mass of citizens."[44] Further, "[A] too-ready method of ascertaining opinion might make government weak rather than strong, foolish, rather than wise."[45]

Rogers also wrote that George Gallup's conceptualization of polling as a continual, rolling referendum on the specific matters of government was a violation of minority rights. The Constitution was not intended to deliver "majority rule pure and simple" as if "the entire country [was] again having a town meeting," but to reach compromises that did not infringe on the rights and privileges of minorities (ethnic, political, and otherwise). Moreover, "Dr. Gallup does not make the public more articulate. . . . He only estimates how in replying to certain questions, it would say 'yes' or 'no' or 'don't know.' Instead of feeling the pulse of democracy, Dr. Gallup listens to its baby talk."[46]

Gallup, ever the evangelical of the religion of polls, responded heatedly in a subsequent letter to *Public Opinion Quarterly*. He called Rogers "perhaps the last of the arm-chair philosophers in the field" and waved him goodbye from the top of his public pedestal: "I, for one, do not begrudge this last—albeit futile—charge by an arm-chair warrior, even if the weapons he chooses are tomahawks and poisonous arrows."[47] And he made the proper rebuttal to Rogers's book: that no pollsters actually believed that statesmen should blindly follow polls. In this response, Gallup highlighted a passage from *The Pulse of Democracy*, written nearly a decade earlier:

> A true statesman will never change his ideals or his principles to make them conform to the opinions of any group, be it large or small. Rather, such a leader will try to persuade the public to accept his views and goals. In fact, his success as a leader will in large part be measured by his success in making converts to his way of thinking.

If this statement seems to stand in opposition to most of George Gallup's other writing, that's because it does. But it was intended to provide cover for the pollsters against some of the sharper criticism at the time *The Pulse of Democracy* was published—and which Rogers resurfaced in 1948. The truth, however, most likely occupies a space between Gallup's and Rogers's arguments. Polls should not be used to blindly dictate the course of the government, and politicians should not ignore information on what their constituents desire. This position has become the "right" one as the country's republican democracy has progressed since the 1940s: as interest groups, lobbyists, and infinitely funded political action committees have grown increasingly powerful over the course of government, polls serve as one of the public's few corrective tools.

Today, the real integration of public opinion into democratic theory fits neither into Rogers's straw-man hypothesis nor Bryce's (via Gallup). Rather, it suggests a broader theoretical framework of how leaders make their decisions. In a 1997 *Public Opinion Quarterly* article titled "Opinion

Quality in Public Opinion Research," Vincent Price and Peter Neijens, two professors of communication and scholars of polling, wrote of the "decision matrix" that can help make sense of how many actors, relying on different sources of information, can come to a collective decision. Price and Neijens formulate an exercise including six groups of actors all participating in a collective decision-making process: political leaders, technical experts, interest groups, newspapers, "attentive publics," and the masses. They are all participants in the process wherein they collectively (1) figure out their own goals, (2) conceptualize their options, (3) estimate the consequences of those actions, and finally (4) make their decision.[48]

We can imagine various stages at which polls could enter our leaders' decision matrices. A modern, middle-of-the-road approach to incorporating public opinion polling into democracy would have political leaders, reporters, and attentive publics consult the polls both when deciding on their goals and when evaluating their options. Issue polls on various policies could help inform legislators which issues are most important to the people, and what outcomes they would prefer. However, polls do not exclusively determine the decision-making process. They are only one input into the several steps of the decision-making process. For example, politicians would be dissuaded from pursuing a policy if polls indicated it was very unpopular, but they might equally decide for or against it if they had strong ideological predispositions toward it. Similarly, a newspaper might decide to pursue an editorial stance (such as writing in favor of corporate trust-busting, for example) that is important to them in part because it is important to the people, but also because the editors and reporters were schooled in the economics of supply and demand and know that monopolies are bad for consumers. Under the Price and Neijens framework, the public's opinions ought only be one part of the calculus that each group of actors is making. Such a reasonable role for polls stands in contrast to integrating them directly into democracy as an omnicompetent, all-powerful actor in the political process.

OVER TIME, ROGERS'S CRITIQUE has faded from the public sphere. Whether we like it or not, the polls are here to stay. Whether because leaders seek out an edge in reelection campaigns or truly care about the public's opinions, they frequently look to (and pay for) them for guidance. It is therefore in citizens' interests to make sure those that do get published are of high methodological caliber and reasonably accurate, rather than attempting to fight off the existence of polls altogether.

Of course, it is reasonable to contend that the public opinion cannot be fully trusted to run the government. Yet it does not, and never will. But opponents of polling often ignore that the data are a useful counter-measure to nefarious actors that would seek to tilt the political scales in their favor—and often away from the public's. As one pollster told me after the 2020 election, in our modern, complex democracy with many participants distorting the path of the government and representation of the people, citizens, reporters, and activists should "grasp at any counter-weights they can find."

3

MACHINE POLITICS

> There is a benign underworld in American politics.... [It]
> is made up of innocent and well-intentioned people who
> work with slide rules and calculating machines and com-
> puters which can retain an almost infinite number of bits
> of information.... [They may] radically reconstruct the
> American political system.
>
> —EUGENE BURDICK, *THE 480*, 1964

Eugene Burdick was an enigma. He was a political scientist and a celebrated novelist, a scuba diver and a model for beer advertisements
(they dubbed him the "Ale Man"). He drank whiskeys with Marlon
Brando and, according to some, might have even been a spy. For a bespec-
tacled professor at the University of California, Berkeley, Burdick lived
a life that was closer to the lives of the characters he imagined for his
several novels.

In 1964, Burdick wrote a book titled *The 480*, a unique work of fiction imagining the journey of an engineer-turned-presidential-candidate

whose handlers abuse the newfound power of early computers to get a leg up on the Republican nomination for the presidency. *The 480* follows a construction manager and engineer named John Thatch as he is recruited by the Republicans to be the charismatic face of a computer-optimized bid for the White House. Much of what Thatch says or does is first run through a computer program that guesses how voters will respond. Thatch is less a politician than the idea of a politician, manufactured by the machines behind a curtain. Thatch's handlers are a mix of conniving, cigar-smoking party bosses and wonky behavioral scientists.

The 480 comes to a climax (and swift close) when John Thatch considers attacking his chief opponent, Dr. Bryant Clark, for dodging the Second World War as a conscientious objector. The computers say that this would win him more convention delegates than he'd lose. In response, Clark's campaign threatens to tell the press that Thatch's Filipino wife prostituted herself to a Japanese prison guard in order to escape captivity. Thatch withdraws from the nomination moments before she throws herself off the Golden Gate Bridge. The novel's message has become a familiar trope in the half-century since Burdick published it: we must not let computers corrupt our humanity.

The 480 is set in its own fictional, dystopian political version of the mid-twentieth century, only loosely based on reality. The 1960 presidential election was the first in which candidates employed modern strategies of social science to "game out" how various decisions might impact voter behavior. John F. Kennedy's campaign hired one such group of behavioral social scientists from the Massachusetts Institute of Technology and Yale who had incorporated their "set of slide rules and calculating machines" into a consulting firm called the Simulmatics Corporation. The researchers analyzed decades of data on individual interviews borrowed from the dusty archives of prominent political pollsters in order to break up the electorate into 480 like groups (hence Burdick's title) that could be used to test different messaging strategies and "optimize" a political campaign, just the way ad men test messages for new products. As the corporation's leading scientists wrote:

> The immediate goal of the project was to estimate rapidly, during the campaign, the probable impact upon the public, and upon small strategically important groups within the public, of different issues which might arise or which might be used by the candidates.

Burdick's book imagines a situation in which American politics has become dominated by an "underworld" of companies similar to Simulmatics. Burdick posited that the future would bring a mass of "innocent and well-intentioned people who work with slide rules and calculating machines" into politics to unwittingly enable nefarious leaders to abuse data as means to their political ends. With the knowledge they could obtain from public opinion polls and computer simulations, they would hand the fate of country over to "the great masses who know very little," rather than "a few who know a great deal."

Some of the anxieties given voice by *The 480* have been validated by history. Citizens around the globe, but in the United States especially, are increasingly commoditized by masses of "big data" about them that are sold to the highest bidder for targeting by retailers and political campaigns; the "underworld" of micro-targeting and psychological profiling is indeed very real; and predictions of how individual Americans might vote have spawned a massive industry of data-driven political consultants who shape the way campaigns make their decisions.

However, time has not smiled upon the novel's too-early conclusions about the perils of data-driven democracy. Much like those of naysayers Walter Lippmann and Lindsay Rogers, Burdick's objections to the integration of polls into government have been damned in history books as an overreaction. "Burdick's dystopianism," the historian Jill Lepore has written, "is vintage Cold War: the Strangelovian fear of the machine. (Burdick also cowrote 'Fail Safe,' in which a computer error triggers a nuclear war.)" And according to Lepore, one review of *The 480* noted that by 1964 Simulmatics was struggling to win enough clients to keep the company afloat (it ended up shutting its doors by 1970). If it couldn't sell leaders on the promises of polling analysis, what was all the fuss about? Even its most famous "success" in 1960, as we will see, may have been little more than slick marketing and other such puffery.[2]

The 480 was successful in large part because it preyed upon elites' worries that firms such as the Simulmatics Corporation—and pollsters such as George Gallup—would take away their influence over political outcomes. They also saw opinion-reading as a potential threat to democracy, arguing that the ability to know how voters would react to a turn of phrase or the adoption of a certain policy position would lead candidates to suspend their judgment and do whatever would please the masses. Soon, politicians wouldn't do what was right, but what was easy and electorally advisable. Burdick's dystopian politicians would take up only those positions that were widely popular. Politics would be dominated by nefarious men who would use algorithms and statistics to corrupt the democratic process in order to empower and enrich themselves. Computers would lead to a blind embrace of the electoral connection, according to Burdick, all in the name of maximizing each candidate's potential to win. Our leaders would do ugly, anti-democratic things in this new political underworld—and with computers on their side, they could get away with it.

Burdick's imaginations conveniently omit several important points. First, an underworld of politics already existed, just without computers. Politicians already played a dirty game of tricks and blackmail. The 1960 election, which motivated Burdick to write *The 480*, was itself notable for allegations of ballot-box stuffing in Chicago. The advent of computers made trickery no more or less likely to sway election outcomes. In fact, anyone in politics could have purchased the "secrets" of Kennedy's 1960 campaign with ease; they were detailed by his campaign manager in a field guide titled "The Democratic Campaign Manual, 1964," which cost a whopping 50 cents at the time (roughly five dollars in 2020 currency).[3]

But Eugene Burdick and his like-minded allies may have made a graver error in not seeing polls as a remedy for the inequalities of our political system. The development, embrace, and evolution of public opinion polling has been one of the most democratizing forces in American political history. Polls are reported on unceasingly by journalists in the mainstream press, as George Gallup himself envisioned. And this chapter later discusses the way they shape decisions for elected officials all the way up to the president. Polls give a voice to the people, especially the marginalized, and in the mid-1900s—as is still true today—the people in power looked very different than those at the bottom. Political surveys are one of the few tools to fight the inevitable stifling of voices that comes along with income and political inequality. Men like Burdick who resisted such democratization on the grounds that the public "knew little" about the particularities of government embraced an outdated and elitist view of self-governance.

The influence of *The 480* over our politics is obviously less pronounced than the opponents of polling and empiricism predicted. Not every campaign consulting firm is a Cambridge Analytica, nor every candidate a John Thatch. In reality, the use of public opinion polling by the political "machine" is much more mundane.

DATA MINING

Consider the story of one Finnish-American man from the bitterly cold Upper Peninsula of Michigan. Born in 1892, Emil Hurja followed many careers. He panned for gold in Fairbanks, Alaska. He published a newspaper in a small oil town in Texas (until a fire burned down the town). He traveled to Europe during World War I as a peace advocate and official representative from Alaska. He was as self-made as they come, an entrepreneur always chasing the next big thing.

In 1928, Emil Hurja found himself in the shining Wall Street offices of a brokerage firm that had hired him to make money investing in mining companies. This was a significant step up from the penniless days of his frontier work; when he first traveled west from

Michigan, Hurja hitched rides on the boxcars of freight trains and ate "mulligan stew" (a dish popular in homeless encampments consisting of whatever ingredients could be procured) with other transient workers. But despite these newfound comforts, he was looking for a new challenge.[4]

That year, Hurja made a pitch to the Democratic National Committee (DNC) to use primitive techniques of statistical sampling—which he learned at lectures from mining experts while in college—to forecast electoral support for the party's presidential nominee, Alfred E. Smith. As he later explained to inquiring newsmen:

> You apply the same test to public opinion that you do to ore. In mining you take several samples from the face of the ore, pulverize them, and find out what the average pay per ton will be. In politics you take sections of voters, check new trends against past performances, establish percentage shift among different voting strata, supplement this information from competent observers in the field, and you can accurately predict an election result.

This description, compelling enough for any young analyst to propose to a modern political candidate's campaign and receive a reasonable position, only got Hurja laughed out of the room. The DNC's chairman, John J. Raskob, dismissed him as a crackpot. Raskob instead preferred to rely on reports from precinct captains and other party operatives to direct their campaign. Smith lost the election.

In the summer of 1932, Emil Hurja again made his case to the DNC's leadership. He alleged that Smith's campaign wasted crucial resources in states that were bound to remain Republican or Democratic and didn't focus enough on the competitive ones. Further, he argued that had the campaign hired him to analyze public opinion data, they would have avoided these mistakes. Hurja proposed to gather a massive number of interviews with voters and combine them with insights from analysts on the ground, dubbed his "Minute Men of the Democratic Party," to devise optimal electoral strategies.[5]

He detailed his precise methods in a longer "Memorandum and Outline" issued to the DNC. Through his "close personal contact" with many (pre-scientific) "pollers," Hurja would gather the data and results of many different polls, often before they were released publicly. He would then compare support for Democratic candidates over time, and against previous election results, to reveal a "picture of sentiment" that reacted to certain campaign events. This "trend analysis" method would allow him to track the success of different campaign events—speeches by politicians, news stories, public policy announcements, and the like. "At any time," Hurja wrote, he could "test the effect of a particular speech of the Candidate or the Opposition with a test poll conducted on the street through our own workers. . . . [P]olls should prove of tremendous value if only to save needless expenditure of campaign funds in districts where not needed."[6]

Further, Hurja proposed to fix the class bias of straw polls such as the ones run by the *Literary Digest* and the Hearst newspapers so that they could be more reliable. By comparing their predictions in previous elections to the actual results, he could compute an average bias in the earlier polls and subtract it from their current ones. If the poll overestimated Democrats by two points last time, he would subtract two points this time. When he could get the underlying data for a poll, Hurja would also re-weight them to make sure that respondents from one city, county, or state did not dominate the others.[7] As crude as these adjustments were, the techniques behind them were novel.

Presented with Hurja's impressive scheme, and worried about their party's candidate again in 1932, the DNC listened. They contracted him as a consultant and placed him under the offices of the new chairman, James Farley. Hurja went to work with his tracking polls and congressional forecasts to support the election of Franklin Delano Roosevelt. In the end, his predictive accuracy was incredible. On November 4, the Friday before the election, Hurja anticipated a "revolution at the ballot box" that would see Roosevelt win by 7.5 million votes. He won by a margin of 7.1. Hurja predicted the right winner in every state except Delaware, Pennsylvania, and Connecticut, where his projection that Roosevelt would win narrowly turned out to be wrong.[8]

Although overlooked by most histories of polling in favor of George Gallup, Louis Harris, and others, Hurja was the real originator of the use of polling analysis for election analysis, and, more importantly, for guiding campaign decisions. For his efforts, the historian Melvin Holli has called him the "driving force" behind the Democrats' dominance during the New Deal era. The political scientist Robert Eisinger wrote that Hurja's work for FDR "signaled the birth of presidential polling . . . and transformed the presidency and American politics."[9]

Others have dubbed him the "Wizard of Washington."

THE WIZARD OF WASHINGTON

Roosevelt and Farley kept Hurja on payroll throughout the next two election cycles, assigning him increasingly influential roles that would help shape some of the specifics of Roosevelt's New Deal—and the future of the country. Farley named Hurja the executive director of the DNC just in time for the 1934 midterm elections, in effect giving him power over the whole organization while Farley was busy performing the duties of the postmaster general.

That year saw Hurja do his most impressive targeting and election-forecasting yet. His analysis of polling data and field reports had become so complex that he not only could tell the DNC which states and congressional districts to spend in, but which individual counties would win or lose a contest. This was the finest-grained data that any political operation had ever had. So wrote Hurja in a report, "Taking ten counties in a certain congressional district—in three of those there is no chance of victory; in three others there is no chance of defeat. Of the remaining four, two are small and two are large. Concentrate on the two largest and the district will be won."[10] When he received polling that revealed the popularity of many New Deal programs, Hurja also urged candidates to emphasize the federal funds that Roosevelt had allocated for their state. For example, after emphasizing a new hydroelectric dam in Passamaquoddy Bay, Maine, Louis J. Brann became the first Democratic governor of the state in over eighty years to win reelection—and it would be twenty more years until Maine Democrats would accomplish such a feat again.[11]

Heading into the November elections, the political commentariat issued its usual prognostications that the party controlling the White House would lose seats in Congress. But Hurja bucked the conventional wisdom, arguing that they would win ten Senate races and actually gain House seats. Of course, he was right. With Hurja translating Roosevelt's New Deal projects into campaign advice, the Democrats won the biggest midterm victory for the party in the White House of the twentieth century—even outranking all of the twenty-first-century midterms so far. James Farley was so impressed with Hurja's forecasts that he dubbed him the "crystal gazer from Crystal Falls."[12]

FROM 1935 ON, Roosevelt appears to have relied directly on his soothsayer to tell him whether his New Deal policies were being received well by the public. By then, Hurja had nearly perfected his own private polling—conducted in part by sending employees of the Works Progress Administration (WPA) to canvas pro– and anti–New Deal sentiment in cities and small towns across America. He had also fine-tuned the statistical adjustments he applied to the pre-publication Gallup and *Literary Digest* polls to make them representative. He used that data to identify which programs the public disliked—namely, the "make work" projects that critics alleged gave easy jobs to projects that weren't worth the funding—and recommended Roosevelt launch a campaign to shore up the WPA's image, or for congressional candidates to distance themselves from it. And when Roosevelt's popularity dipped in 1935 after the Supreme Court invalidated some of his policies and he went on an angry "tirade" against big business, Hurja noticed that his approval rating dipped, so he recommended he relax his rhetoric and change course. Roosevelt relented, according to Holli, the historian who wrote the book on Hurja, and his approval recovered.[13]

In 1935, Farley asked Hurja to run a "secret" poll of Roosevelt's vulnerability in the next year's election. Roosevelt had become privately concerned about a third-party challenge from a Louisiana senator named Huey Long, who was gaining publicity with a program for universal income called "Share Our Wealth" and had the rallying cry "Every Man a King." Who wouldn't vote for that?

Hurja's poll found that Long was attracting the support of 3 or 4 million potential voters, primarily Democratic ones. He presented the results to Roosevelt over dinner one evening, apparently causing the president to become "jumpy" at his own very imaginable defeat.[14] By the fall, a *Literary Digest* poll showed Roosevelt with a 63% disapproval rating.

By 1936, Emil Hurja had become famous in Washington for his accurate forecasts. In March, *Time* printed his face on the cover of their magazine—twelve years and two months before they bestowed the same accolade on George Gallup. Not only did he shape some of the foundational policies of the twentieth century, he also steered the press's election coverage. These two machines—politics and the press—were bowing to the Wizard of Washington, the "soothsayer" and "magic forecaster."[15]

It was around that time when Hurja started conducting regular "scientific" private polls. His personal papers record numerous conversations with George Gallup, including Hurja's discovery of the first straw polls in 1824 that Gallup would use in his 1940 book with Saul Forbes Rae.[16] The methodological rigor of Hurja's scientific poll may have even exceeded Gallup's. His first poll of the 1936 election in early February was mailed to 1,000 people, grouped (or "stratified") by region and population density, so that he did not survey too many northern city-dwellers or southern farmers. In a document for a poll in Michigan, G. D. Kennedy, one of Hurja's correspondents and the manager of the State Highway Commission, explained that he randomly sampled every fiftieth voter in each county off a list of automobile owners, ensuring a fair geographic portrait of voters that attenuated some (but not all) of the class bias that plagued the *Literary Digest* straw polls. Upon Hurja's direction, the poll was also weighted so that the vote choices of respondents who had voted in the 1932 election matched the documented election results in the state.[17]

Hurja also used his "trend analysis" method to compare polls taken immediately before and after Roosevelt gave a speech. Reporting on his studies conducted while the president was on a late-campaign tour around the country, he told Roosevelt that the poll taken "two days after your visit" to a series of Midwestern towns showed an increase in support of "13.9% taking the same number of the same type of samples in each city, before and after your visit."[18]

Weeks later, Roosevelt won the election, again proving the soundness of Emil Hurja's then-state-of-the-art "scientific" polls. He joined George Gallup, Elmo Roper, and Archibald Crossley in trouncing the *Digest*.

IN 1937, EMIL HURJA LEFT the Roosevelt administration. With three successful election predictions under his belt, and somewhat put off by the president's court-packing plan that year, he entered private practice. He worked first for the Walgreen Drug Company, then revisited election projections for various congressional, senatorial, and gubernatorial candidates during the 1938 midterms—some of them Republicans.[19]

Hurja purchased the nearly bankrupt *Pathfinder* magazine in 1939, using it to raise support for Finland during its invasion by Russia in World War II and as a vehicle for publicizing his polls. Just before the 1940 election, he wrote up a report on an October poll with the headline MIGHTY CLOSE, BUT THE RACE IS STILL WILLKIE'S. Wendell Willkie, the Republican nominee for president, lost the election to Roosevelt by a ten-point margin. The magazine actually survived the debacle, but struggled financially until Hurja sold most of his stake in 1943.

Hurja's *Pathfinder* poll faltered again in 1948, predicting that Truman would lose to Thomas Dewey. But unlike George Gallup four years later, Hurja did not recover. Infuriated by the missed prediction and inundated with angry letters from subscribers, Graham Patterson, the new publisher of the magazine, sent Hurja packing. He went back to consulting, and managed to field more accurate polls than the more popular public pollsters in 1952, but never again enjoyed the same influence. He died of a heart attack in 1953, at the age of 61.[20]

EMIL HURJA IS FORGOTTEN by most. But his "trend analysis" and early adoption of quota controls and "scientific polling" shaped how political party committees allocated resources in campaigns, and how presidents governed. Roosevelt, the first president with a pollster, used Hurja's data for two main purposes. He used the data to direct his efforts to hand out residual federal funds where they would be the most useful, and he also used polls as a corrective when he strayed too far from the public mandate for his governing. In 1935, the Supreme Court invalidated the National Industrial Recovery Act and Agricultural Adjustment Act—two acts establishing organizations to regulate state commerce—as unconstitutional usurpations of state power. Hurja told the president that his polls showed that most Americans opposed the power-centralizing acts anyway, and that he should move on or find a different means toward the same guiding policy.[21] (Roosevelt pushed a new version of the latter act in 1938, so it's unclear how much he listened to his soothsayer on this occasion.)

The early history of data used by the president, then, tells a story of a constraining rather than a tyrannical role for the nerds. This runs contrary to the doomsday expectations of Eugene Burdick and his sympathizers.

THE PEOPLE MACHINE

In the decades between Emil Hurja's departure from the Roosevelt administration in 1937 and John F. Kennedy's announcement of his presidential bid in 1960, the use of polls by political campaigns and committees evolved very little. But a group of social scientists from MIT, Columbia, Harvard, and Yale had been preparing for their moment in the sun. This was the year, they hoped, that they would fundamentally transform politics forever.

Ithiel de Sola Pool, an MIT political scientist, was the brains of the Simulmatics Corporation. Ed Greenfield, a Madison Avenue advertising executive and frequent supporter of Democratic politicians, was its salesman. Working together, the two recruited a team of political scientists and computer programmers to compile polling data and create a computer program that would predict how certain policy positions would affect their candidate's election prospects. A piece written for *Harper's Magazine* later described Simulmatics' efforts to create their so-called people machine as "the A-bomb of the social sciences."[22]

At the time, Pool's creation must have been alarming in its claims to predict the course of the election before anyone had even been introduced to the candidates, let alone their political promises and likely courses of action. But looking back, the abilities of Pool's statistical machinery were not as impressive as people thought, and even less consequential than Simulmatics claimed. The truth of the endeavor lay principally in the limits of the data available to the researchers, the willingness of Simulmatics' clients to listen to its recommendations, and the novelty of the recommendations themselves.

Simulmatics' formulas ran on polling data and, to a lesser extent, election returns from 1952 on. Its programmers would take interviews conducted by pollsters such as Gallup and Roper, encode the information—about the demographic profiles of each respondent, whether they supported civil rights, and which party they voted for in 1952 or 1956, for example—and feed it into a computer. At the time, the state-of-the-art "calculating machine" (as they were called before "computer" was adopted) was the IBM 704 Data Processing System, which received instructions from a large, thick paper card that had been punched out to encode certain instructions in the Fortran computer language. One card would establish the length of a list of values for a person, 1 through 10, for example. The next would specify the value of the first attribute—perhaps they were a female voter—and so on. An operator would feed the machine, which was composed of many circuits and other hardware spread across a dozen or so metal cabinets, as many cards as it took to complete the program.

The operators could then ask the computer to run a series of mathematical equations using the information on all of those voters. They could look at what happens if there are more Black voters, for example, voting for the Democrats. One question of interest was the impact of a Democratic candidate giving a full-throated endorsement of civil rights among white voters versus Black voters, southern versus northern. Pitching the analytical power of their simulations to the Democratic National Committee in 1959, Greenfield and Pool wrote:

> We will, from our model, be able to predict what such a speech would mean to each of 1,000 sub-groups of the population, and how many individuals belonging to each sub-group there are in each state. We would therefore be able to predict the approximate small fraction of a percent difference that such a speech would make in each state and consequently to pinpoint the state where it could affect the electoral vote. We might thus advise, for example, that such a speech would lose 2 to 3% of the vote in several Southern states that we would carry anyhow, but might gain ½ of a percent of the vote in some crucial Northern state.[23]

The DNC was evidently impressed with the pitch. They gave Pool, Greenfield, and their colleague Bill McPhee, from Columbia's Bureau of Applied Social Research, $35,000 (a little under $240,000 in 2020 dollars) to answer their questions about Black voters.[24]

The team also received a grant from McPhee's colleague Paul Lazarsfeld, a pioneer in the study of voter behavior whose theories were put to work by Simulmatics. Lazarsfeld's prior analyses of polls and community surveys had revealed that voters changed their minds mainly based on "brand loyalties" that forced them toward the Democratic or Republican candidate between election cycles. Religion, social class, and interactions with friends of the same political leaning were among the most influential factors.[25]

The Simulmatics staff theorized that the influence of these forces could be captured by sorting voters into many different "types" based on their political, demographic, and geographic attributes and looking at their average levels of support for a candidate or a policy. As they wrote:

> In the North rural people, upper-income people, Protestants, and...older people tend to be Republicans. Urban people, poor people, Catholics, Jews and...Negroes and young people tend to be Democrats.... However, when social milieu and political views are out of balance, then further adjustment processes may be set in motion. The voter may compromise his views toward those of his friends, or attempt to convince his friends of the merit of his own views.[26]

This theory forms the basis of the company's "simulations" of elections. First, they would start with the share of votes that went to Democrats among each "type" of voter, as defined by the combination of their demographic attributes. One type of voter might be "Eastern, metropolitan, lower-income, white, Catholic, female, Democrat." Then, for the population of persuadable or "cross-pressured" voters—Lazarsfeld's term for someone who held attitudes that were in conflict with each other, or behaved in a contradictory way, such as being a pro–civil rights white southern Democrat—they would make a prediction of Kennedy's vote share by adding together the share of the vote that group cast for Democrats in the last election and the share who favored his course of action; then they would subtract the number of Democratic voters in that group who opposed it. Simulmatics hoped that the difference between Kennedy's vote share in the simulations where he did and did not embrace civil rights could help the candidate decide which course of action to take—and, thus, to hire them.

In May 1960, the team sent their "Negro Votes in Northern Cities" report over to the Kennedy campaign. They had identified the political importance of African American voters in New York, Pennsylvania, California, Illinois, Ohio, Michigan, New Jersey, and Missouri—states that controlled 210 of the 537 electoral votes needed to win the White House—and poked and prodded the data to discern Black voters' responsiveness to civil rights legislation. They reported that it was "the image of what each party had done for the Negro people" that would determine which party the majority voted for. By taking a stronger stance on civil rights, Simulmatics concluded, Kennedy could win over enough cross-pressured, would-be-Republican African Americans to win the election.[27]

In August, after Kennedy won the Democratic nomination for president, he hired Simulmatics to conduct another study. By then, both the campaign and its new scientists had identified another key issue for the general election campaign: whether Kennedy should make a point of defending his Catholicism, which made him the target of attacks by Republicans and Protestant Democrats alike, or ignore the issue altogether. Kennedy had been torn all along. On the one hand, he figured that a defense could win him the support of Catholic Republicans and carry him over the electoral line. But he feared that raising the issue could increase its salience among would-be Democratic defectors.

The problem was perfect for Simulmatics. Running the numbers, they found that Kennedy had already lost most of the voters who would abandon him "if the campaign became embittered by the issue of anti-Catholicism. . . . The net worst has already been done."[28] Therefore, they said, he should embrace the issue and try to win the votes of as many potential Republican Catholics as possible. In September, Pool and

McPhee also advised Kennedy on a strategy for his upcoming debate, telling him to come off strong, competent, and understandable to the average American.[29]

Kennedy proceeded as Simulmatics advised. After the votes for president were tallied, he ended up winning 34,226,731 voters to Richard Nixon's 34,108,157—a popular vote margin of 118,574 votes. It was one of the closest contests ever. And since, in close contests, small changes can have enormous differences, there is all the reason in the world to think that Simulmatics made a difference.

LEADING, OR FOLLOWING?

The picture inside Jack Kennedy's campaign was more complicated. There were too many players, too many sources of information, to be able to discern causality with any semblance of accuracy.

To make matters worse, Kennedy himself did not reveal the precise balancing of evidence for campaign decisions in any diary entries or recorded conversations with his advisors. Even Pool and his partners Robert Abelson and Samuel Popkin could not say. "John F. Kennedy in particular not only understood enough to trust research," they wrote in their 1965 recap of their efforts on his campaign, "he also understood enough to know when and in what respects to distrust it. . . . Our own contribution, if any, was to bolster by evidence one set of alternatives. . . . [W]hen Kennedy decided to confront the bigots head on, he himself could not say what part in his decision was played by any one piece of evidence."[30]

It is hard to parse the fact from the fiction of Simulmatics' account. As they wrote their official account of their work only after Eugene Burdick had so publicly scolded their company in 1964, they may have felt pressure to downplay their influence over Kennedy. But additional anecdotal accounts of Kennedy's dealing with his pollster, Louis Harris, suggest that there may have been some truth to Pool, Abelson, and Popkin's telling of the story.

Louis Harris was a protege of Elmo Roper, but he left that firm to start his own in 1956. Over the span of his career he polled for hundreds of political candidates. But according to one account, not everyone appreciated his insights. "Harris's success is built on an illusion," Michael Wheeler wrote about the pollster's influence over Kennedy in his 1976 book, *Lies, Damn Lies, and Statistics: The Manipulation of Public Opinion in America*. "The quality of the polls he did for Kennedy was spotty at best, and, in the end, Kennedy gave his surveys very little weight. . . . privately [the Kennedys] laughed behind his back."[31] The argument is fair enough; Harris's polls in the Democratic primary were significantly off the mark in Wisconsin and West Virginia, and in the general election he called Ohio, Wisconsin, and Washington for Kennedy—states that all ended up going to Nixon.[32] As pollsters are often penalized for their mistakes of prediction, it would not be surprising if Kennedy had in fact largely ignored Harris.

However, it may have been stranger for Kennedy to keep paying Harris if he did not value him at all. It is more likely that the candidate kept Harris around to help shore up his public image, as well as to assess the salience of certain issues such that he could tailor his speeches and debate performances—but not to find new positions for the candidate or give campaign-changing advice. In 1994, the political scientists Lawrence Jacobs and Robert Shapiro looked at the relationship between Kennedy's speeches and Louis Harris's poll numbers, finding that "the issues that were raised in [the] polls were persistently mentioned by Kennedy in his subsequent public statements." Between September and November, Kennedy took public stances on an average of 56% of issues that poll respondents said were important to them, versus 27% of all the other issues mentioned throughout the campaign. As Jacobs and Shapiro wrote:

> For instance, a more than twofold increase in public support for Medicare during mid-September (from 9% to 22%) coincided— two weeks later—with both a sevenfold increase in Kennedy's daily

attention to the issue (from a policy statement score of 2 to a score of 14) and a decision to select Medicare for exceptionally frequent, strong, and extensive statements during the first debate.[33]

The polling results do not directly suggest that Kennedy took positions because the public wanted him to do so—for example, that public support caused him to favor expanding Medicare—but rather that the campaign focused on the candidate's popular positions and attributes in order to "prime" the average voter's positive evaluations and increase Kennedy's support. Although polls provided a more empirical basis for this strategy, it is no different than how campaigns had worked in the past, or the advice that a "normal" campaign advisor would have given.

Pollsters also offered advice on non-policy issues, and because he was concerned that Kennedy was susceptible to attacks about his youthful appearance, Harris urged his candidate to highlight his maturity, appear "warmer," and slow down the pace of his speaking. An estimated 70 million people may have watched the first 1960 presidential debate, and it is widely assumed that Kennedy's dominant performance over a lackluster and (infamously) perspiring Nixon helped him win the presidency. If Kennedy did craft his debate strategy in response to the polls, he could have been listening to either Ithiel Pool or Louis Harris—or the many advisors and voices in his head who were urging the same course of action. Short of surfacing undiscovered notes in Kennedy's archived papers, it is impossible to know who should earn credit for the advice.

NOBODY CAN ARGUE that the Simulmatics Corporation was not an influential company. Its debut on the New York Stock Exchange in 1961 raised nearly $200,000—or just over $1.75 million in 2020 dollars.[34] Pool and Popkin, among others, would go on to do election-prediction work for the *New York Times* and insurgency-prediction simulations for the United States government in Vietnam. As if this were not enough, the company's contemporaneous impacts on popular culture alone could prove its stature. *Harper's Magazine,* the *New York Herald,* the *Chicago Sun-Times,* and many smaller papers all commented on the company's role in Kennedy's campaign after his victory—calling the company's simulations a "secret weapon" and "atomic bomb" of social science.[35] The "People-Machine," as it was dubbed in the *Harper's* piece, was recognized as a revolutionary step in the study of human behavior—which it certainly was—and in political campaigning—which it was not.

But both the Simulmatics Corporation's publicists and its critics made much more out of its accomplishments, especially in 1960, than a detailed account of their records suggests is accurate. The fear of a political underworld of nerds wielding slide rules and anti-democratic theories turned out, as Jill Lepore wrote nearly sixty years after the fact, to be quite Strangelovian indeed.

IF YOU CAN'T BEAT 'EM, JOIN 'EM

It would take eight years for Richard Nixon to recover fully from his razor-thin defeat by Jack Kennedy in 1960. In the interim years, he unsuccessfully ran to become the governor of California, and then joined a law firm in New York. But in 1968 he finally won the White House. In his first term as president, he was a man struck by pollsters.

Richard Nixon was both a voracious consumer and a constant commissioner of public opinion polls. Only days after his inauguration, he directed his staff to set up a "system" of monitoring the polls so they could figure out "what moves and concerns the average guy." The system included dispatches from private pollsters who took a "quick reading [of public opinion] now, overall and on specific issues." The polls were then circulated among his closest advisors and often discussed at length. Nixon's chief of staff, H. R. Haldeman, wrote in his diary that he met with the president about the state of public opinion at least once a week until his departure in April 1973.[36]

Between 1969 and 1972, the Nixon White House commissioned at least 233 private polls—significantly more than Lyndon Johnson's White House did in his entire six-year presidency. Most were conducted by Nixon's pollster David Derge, though the administration did rely on fifty or so additional reports from a number of other pollsters and organizations whose interests generally aligned with Nixon's.[37] The president used the data both for electoral purposes and to figure out when he had overstepped the public's appetite for a particular political or policy issue; but he also began consulting the data when both drafting and implementing policies.

Nixon sounded particularly Gallup-esque in his orientation toward polling, arguing that regularly conducted issue polls should be used in "running the government" and remain a "permanent concern to the White House, rather than just during elections." In time, Nixon had Derge fielding "telephone quicky polls" on a "number of specific issues" in order to "get immediate response . . . [and] some guidance." Nixon's White House was especially concerned with the trends in the data; their focus was on "producing comparative results from trend analysis," Haldeman said roughly two decades after his service to Nixon. The polls tracked reactions to policy proposals relating to Vietnam, taxes, the Strategic Arms Limitation Talks (SALT), inflation, and other matters. Due in part to the high rates at which people answered telephone pollsters in the '70s, Derge could have a completed sample back to the White House within two days after receiving the request.[38]

Obsessed with his image, Nixon asked his pollsters to identify issues where the public and White House were out of step with each other, and set up public relations responses to avoid backlash. He also identified areas where the public was on his side, and hammered the press if they were covering him negatively. This was not uncommon for presidents to do; Lyndon Johnson famously watched three television sets simultaneously to monitor the news networks and read all the newspapers to identify areas of weakness. Similarly, Nixon wanted his staff to "know what we must do to counteract whatever effect [media coverage] may be having on public opinion."[39]

Nixon also used polling data to make publicly sanctioned decisions about executive strategy and government policy. In this way, polls became a tool of populist governance, increasing the congruence of Washington's policy outputs with the general will of the majority. Harry Dent, one of Nixon's political advisors, said in 1993 that "Nixon would not have taken an initiative on any particular areas without looking at some [polling] statistics.... Nixon did not fly through planet earth by the seat of his britches."[40]

Although he circulated issue polls widely within the administration, Nixon considered the polls of his popularity, general election standings, and personal image to be particularly sensitive subject matter. According to one source, Nixon "sought to portray himself as a 'courageous President ... [who] fights for what he believes [is "right" for the country] regardless of the political consequences.'" He yearned to be thought of both as an expert statesman and a "prime strategist"—a "political genius" who "didn't need to go by public opinion polls" in order to be popular. And though his image today is tainted by his involvement with the Watergate scandal—and the larger nefariousness of the Committee to Re-Elect the President (CREEP), organized under Nixon's campaign operation rather than placed directly in the White House—many forget that he was very popular. Nixon's job approval rating in George Gallup's polls usually hovered above 60%. Nevertheless, he had Haldeman lock up his polls in his office safe and keep them away from the prying eyes of many of his cabinet members and other advisors, who he feared might leak them to the press and undermine his credibility.[41]

For the 1972 campaign, Nixon hired a young strategist and poll-savvy analyst named Robert Teeter to focus on his reelection efforts. Teeter was a whiz among his peers, skilled (for his time) in statistical methods. He could run spatial and multivariate regressions—advanced techniques that pollsters from earlier generations could not easily perform—on survey data, and used focus groups to gauge audience evaluations of presidential statements, in addition to the tried-and-true methods of trend analysis that allowed candidates to detect actions that helped or hurt their support. Teeter also developed a system so CREEP could analyze voting data all the way to the precinct level, allowing campaign operatives to direct hyper-localized resources to boost Nixon's chances. Teeter fully modernized the methods of polling analysis available to CREEP. He would go on to use the same tools for Ronald Reagan's and George H. W. Bush's campaigns for president.[42]

Nixon was reelected in 1972 with 61% of the popular vote, versus 38% for his opponent, George McGovern. The White House had seen the victory coming months back. So too did the public pollsters; George Gallup and Louis Harris (who had now suspended his private practice to focus on public polling) pegged the contest at 62–38 and 61–39 for Nixon and McGovern, respectively.[43] The last decade of methodological improvements helped pollsters put errors on the scale of the 1948 misfire behind them. Such accuracy is attributable, in large part, to Washington's increasing appetite for survey data.

THE TRUTH IS OUT THERE

It is impossible to precisely quantify the effects of polling on government leaders. Too much is unknowable. For example, did Franklin Roosevelt's patronage positions for loyal members of Congress actually increase his electoral fortunes in targeted areas? Did Jack Kennedy make his decisions based on the Simulmatics Corporation's modeling, or because of the polls? Or did he shape his campaign in spite of both? Did the use of polls increase Richard Nixon's approval rating by one percentage point, or ten? Did his odds of defeating McGovern increase by so much that polls handed him reelection when he would have otherwise lost? What level of government funding in specific policy areas can be attributed directly to the polls?

Though historians can conduct case studies of archived government records, diary entries, and other conversations that suggest a causal link between polls and policy, we may never know the true magnitude of the relationship. But the decisions that Nixon made on the backs of his pollsters may have nevertheless been very consequential. For example, before making his decision to withdraw US troops from Vietnam, Nixon reportedly kept track of trends in public opinion—something that his predecessor Lyndon Johnson did not do, potentially costing tens of thousands of American lives. The president's decision to campaign for China's admission to the United Nations was made in a similar fashion.[44]

Accordingly, the 1970s and 1980s saw the partial realization of George Gallup's vision for a government that maintained a closer relationship with the people through the continuous monitoring of their collective will. For the first time, polls were officially institutionalized in the offices of the White House. Various case studies suggest that polls constrained the actions of Richard Nixon—and, to a lesser extent, presidents Jimmy Carter and Ronald Reagan after him—when his image sank, and emboldened him when the public issued directions both on which issues to focus on and how to address them.

To be sure, the example from Nixon's White House—and the four elected twentieth-century presidents who followed him—also showed that politicians can use polls to manipulate the public. They can avoid accountability for some bad actions, or to launch ambitious public relations campaigns to increase support for their actions on issues with low salience among the public. But history has shown that they can only get away with so much. Usually, the people ask for their due.

THE INHERENT POPULISM of public opinion research has been a net benefit to the people. Leaders tend to change course when their approval ratings dip, and continue on course when they soar. But this does not mean opinion research is always perfectly conducted, or even always deployed to the public's benefit. As with any scientific enterprise, polling is not immune to errors of human judgment. And as with any tool for good, there are also examples of people using polling for bad.

4

ONE BAD APPLE DOESN'T SPOIL THE BUSHEL

There are three kinds of lies: lies, damned lies, and statistics.

—MARK TWAIN AND OTHERS

Despite the enormous promise of public opinion polls, they are not without their faults. As the many historical examples of pre-election forecasts have shown, pollsters can make errors both of art and science, small and large. The assumptions of stability in candidate preferences made in advance of the 1948 election, for example, show how human error can contaminate the process of surveying people and talking about their attitudes. More recently, problems in the 2016 and 2020 presidential elections showed how the actual statistical tools of the polls can break down in unpredictable ways.

Some of these errors of polling are typical problems of the evolution of any science. The history of polling, like that of other new technologies, has been one of trial and error. Pollsters have acknowledged their mistakes, fixed them, and gone on to create better devices for taking the public's pulse.

Other problems in the polls have been a product of the times in which they were conducted. In the 1930s and '40s, for example, Jim Crow laws in the South effectively prevented African Americans from voting. In pursuit of more accurate election forecasts, George Gallup did not establish a minimum number of Black voters in the states—he was averse to "Negro quotas" in his polls.[1] As a result, the claims of a poll-driven utopia, where the voices of all Americans no matter their class, color, or creed were, in hindsight, demonstrably incorrect. Who surveyors talk to, what they ask them, and the numbers of each group they assume to be in the overall population all impact a poll's eventual results.

The good news is that the public opinion profession has been responsive to this kind of critique. The dedication to the various tools of survey research, as well as the belief in the equality they afford the people, has perpetually pushed the industry toward a brighter future. It will likely continue to do so; despite the challenges they have faced, researchers have always found ways to improve their instruments.

But polling is vulnerable to some more severe infractions. There are pollsters who work for unsavory clients, using interviews as a tool to push respondents to one outcome or the other. Rather than taking the public's pulse, these pollsters raise it. Others are driven by fame or ideological motivations to cling to bad methods. And there are those who invent or distort their data altogether—a common technique, as we'll see, is to duplicate a valid interview with one individual many times over. Though they represent a fraction of the industry, members of this dark underbelly of survey research have contaminated polls for clients that include small academic institutions, major public survey organizations, and even the United States Department of State.

Skeptics believe that these bad apples spoil the whole bunch. And while many companies that conduct surveys (of which political, pre-election, and other public opinion polls are generally thought of as a subset, though pollsters often use the terms interchangeably) conform to conventional standards of methodology and transparency, those that don't risk giving the public the impression that all public opinion polls are equally faulty. This chapter discusses several of the largest scandals and gravest errors in political polling over the last fifty years. These are aberrant examples of methodological failure; but if pollsters do not acknowledge the shortcomings of the tools they use, they are doomed to repeat their mistakes.

DEATH AND SANCTIONS IN IRAQ

On May 12, 1996, CBS News journalist Lesley Stahl interviewed the US ambassador to the United Nations, Madeleine Albright, for a program on the impacts of UN economic sanctions against Iraq. The segment, called "Punishing Saddam," ran on the popular news show *60 Minutes*. While pictures of Iraqi mothers holding starving children scrolled across the screen, Stahl cited a shocking figure from a new academic study: according to surveys out of Iraq, the sanctions that the UN had put in place following Iraq's invasion of Kuwait had killed roughly 500,000 Iraqi children. "We have heard that a half million children have died," Stahl said. "I mean, that's more children than died in Hiroshima. And, you know, is the price worth it?"

Albright waffled over an answer. As the camera panned to her, she said, "I think this is a very hard choice, but the price—we think the price is worth it." Stahl won an Emmy for the segment, a highlight of her career. But while Albright's answer didn't cause any immediate shock waves to ripple through the media (there are some accounts that college students later protested her visits because of the segment), it would turn out to be one of the more embarrassing mistakes of her career.

Albright's mistake was not her fault. Analysis conducted after the program aired revealed that the study Stahl cited was based on very problematic data. The interviews of Iraqi households that had been given to researchers were tainted by significant biases—and may have even been fabricated to sway public opinion.

I AM SITTING across from Michael Spagat in a sunny coffee shop in South Bank, about an hour-long train ride from his offices at Royal Holloway, University of London. Spagat is originally from Chicago, but has been living and working in London since 1997. He earned his degree in economics from Harvard in 1988 studying Soviet central planning, but after the breakup of the USSR he pivoted to studying the economics of war.

In the late 2000s, Spagat found "inconsistencies"—academic speak for evidence of potentially fabricated data—in many different surveys in the Middle East. Unofficial estimates of death rates in Iraq during the 1990s, he alleges, are almost all based on exaggerated or manufactured polling data. One author responsible for the 1996 study that Lesley Stahl used in her Emmy Award–winning interview with Secretary Albright even partially retracted the work "for serious replication problems," according to Spagat.

The study had been conducted by two researchers for the Food and Agriculture Organization, a UN agency that works to combat hunger around the world. One of the report's authors, Sarah Zaidi, worked for the Center for Social and Economic Rights, a nonprofit in New York City. Her coauthor, Dr. Mary Smith Fawzi, was working for the Harvard University School of Public Health at the time. The scientists based their research on two surveys they oversaw, one completed in 1991 and the other in 1995, both consisting of face-to-face interviews with randomly selected households in and around Baghdad. They did physical exams of children to assess malnutrition, and asked mothers how many children they had lost. In December 1995, they wrote up their conclusions and submitted them in a letter to the *Lancet*, the journal of the British Medical Association. Comparing the mortality and nutrition data from 1995 to the corresponding 1991 figures, the researchers concluded that any differences were due to the UN's sanctions, and claimed that between August 1990 and December 1995, "567,000 children in Iraq have died as a consequence."

Spagat says that "the contention that sanctions caused half a million child deaths is very likely to be wrong." In the first place, it is impossible to ascribe causality for the increased deaths to the sanctions alone. Any number of other factors—drought, maybe, or even political violence—could have caused additional variation in the death rate. But it is also hard to believe the researchers' data could accurately reflect child death rates overall in Iraq. Because the Iraqi government did not keep accurate surveys of child death statistics, any country-wide estimates would have to be based on extrapolations from smaller populations. In making such extrapolations, a researcher risks projecting sampling errors onto the whole population.

According to Spagat, the problem with the Iraq child mortality study probably lies in this extrapolation. When survey statisticians conduct a household survey, they typically make a random selection of households in an area to visit and ensure that different parts of the area—be it a city, a state, or a country—are proportionally represented in the sample. In a child mortality study, for example, the researcher would then interview all women living in the selected households who are between the ages of 15 and 49 and who have given birth within the time period covered by the survey. "Best practice is to take full birth histories for each mother," Spagat outlines, "including dates of birth and death . . . for each of her children. This information is then used to estimate age- and time-specific mortality rates" for the entire population.[2]

But Spagat's public questions about Zaidi and Fawzi's paper raised suspicions about the household interviews they used and the calculations they made to arrive at their eye-popping mortality rate. One letter to the *Lancet* in 1996 prompted Zaidi to return to Iraq to verify the survey data herself. She found that many households could not confirm deaths that the government-supplied field teams had originally reported.[3] So she asked the *Lancet* to retract their study in 1997. What, then, was the error? In a 2010 journal article published in *Significance*, the journal of Britain's Royal Statistical Society, Spagat reported Zaidi's speculation that " 'some' Iraqi surveyors recorded deaths when they did not take place or the child had died outside the time frame but they specified the opposite."

If such fabrication did indeed take place, why would people have lied? They may have faced the age-old problem of "interviewer effect," where respondents change their answers based on who is asking the question. Zaidi and Fawzi's conclusion that mortality rates had increased was based on changes between two surveys, one from 1991 and another from 1995. But these surveys were supervised by different organizations and the interviews were conducted by different workers. While the 1991 survey was supervised by Harvard University, and interviews were conducted both by Iraqi locals and college students from nearby Jordan, the 1995 study was conducted by the Iraqi government. Since Saddam Hussein's regime was interested in exaggerating the toll of the sanctions to get them repealed, this could have made all the difference.

According to Spagat, "Iraq's citizens feared the Iraqi regime which, in turn, clearly wanted its citizens to tell surveyors that they had suffered many child deaths. Respondents to surveys in Iraq might easily have suspected that their confidentiality could be breached to the regime, in which case they could have been punished for not reporting enough child deaths." Further, although there is no way to be sure, the Iraqi government could have also instructed the interviewers—government employees—to report more deaths than they were told about. "In short," Spagat wrote, "Iraqis in various positions relative to the survey all had incentives to inflate Iraq's child mortality rates."

More suggestive evidence that the Iraqi government may have indirectly or directly tainted its surveys shows up in a separate study of child mortality sponsored by UNICEF and supervised by Kurdish leaders, who (at the time) lived in northern Iraq in a largely autonomous region outside the influence of the central government. But in the area of the country controlled by Saddam Hussein, he used his own workers for the survey. So interviewers trained separately by Kurdish and Iraqi government authorities fielded the Iraq Child and Maternal Mortality Survey (ICMMS) in February and March of 1999. The surveys showed child mortality doubling in south and central Iraq from 1990 to 1992, whereas it only increased by 30% in the Kurdish zone.

"This is puzzling," Spagat says, since the sanctions applied to the entire country. According to one account from an Iraqi doctor, speaking after coalition forces toppled Saddam Hussein's government in 2003, the type of manipulation needed to explain these numbers was rampant in the country at the time. "This was not a country where people disagreed," he said.[4]

In 2005, 2007, and 2008, the United Nations backed three new independent surveys of child mortality rates in Iraq. Each of them recalculated deaths going back in time. None showed evidence of a large increase in child death rates following the UN's sanctions in 1991.

MISSION ACCOMPLISHED?

In 2010, seven years after he joined US-led efforts to invade Iraq, UK prime minister Tony Blair testified before a government committee investigating his role in the conflict (called the Iraq Inquiry, or the Chilcot Inquiry, after the investigation's chairman, Sir John Chilcot) to offer justification for his decisions. The officials in charge of the investigation, most of them current and former members of Parliament, demanded to know why the UK's interest in removing Saddam Hussein from power justified the 2003 invasion.

The morning of January 29, Blair walked into the committee's chambers in the Queen Elizabeth II Centre across the street from London's iconic Westminster Abbey and testified for nearly seven hours. It was an unconvincing performance, according to the inquiry's eventual report. Among other charges, Blair's case for war was inadequate, and he did not exhaust all peaceful options before joining the United States in Iraq.

In terms of the Iraq War, none of this is particularly remarkable. Investigators in the United Kingdom, the United States, and elsewhere have long known of the coalition's charades to justify an invasion. But in terms of the surveys of Iraqi child mortality, which had been shown to be compromised as early as 2007, Blair's testimony was everything. In a particularly revealing set of comments, the former prime minister stated that one of his justifications for the war was that child mortality had dropped after the forces toppled Hussein's regime:

> In 2000 and 2001 and 2002 [Iraq] had a child mortality rate of 130 per 1,000 children under the age of five, worse than the Congo. That was despite the fact that Saddam had as much money as he wanted for immunisation programmes and medicines for those children. That equates to roughly about 90,000 deaths under the age of five a year. The figure today is not 130, it is 40. That equates to about 50,000 young people, children, who, as a result of a different regime that cares about its people—that's the result that getting rid of Saddam makes.[5]

As Michael Spagat's series of sobering reports has revealed, no quality survey has ever found mortality rates in Iraq of 130 per 1,000 children. The UN's set of three independent, verified surveys uncovered rates closer to 30–40 per 1,000. The only claim of death rates as high as 130 per 1,000 is traced back to the retracted *Lancet* study coauthored by Mary Fawzi and Sarah Zaidi and the demonstrably errant interviewing of the Iraqi government itself—both aligned with groups that sought to curtail the UN's economic sanctions against Iraq in the 1990s.

Polls based on flawed data can have massive consequences for those who are unaware of their faulty inner workings. The Chilcot report also shows how bad actors will cling to low-quality data to support their conclusions even long after these have been decried by the survey industry and statistical community—or, in Sarah Zaidi's case, even the survey's primary researcher.

MANUFACTURING CONSENT

Although the data that is collected in the vast majority of polls can be verified, data fabrication has historically been a serious problem, especially in non-western countries. One of the most famous examples also comes from Iraq, and Michael Spagat again revealed the widespread deficiencies in data that would be widely relied upon by the US government.

In a study for the *Lancet*, epidemiologist Gilbert Burnham surveyed Iraqi households on the number of people they know who suffered violent deaths between March 2003 and July 2006. He concluded the conflict was killing 180,000 people each year—roughly 490 people each day. To Spagat, this finding was an astronomical outlier. It would have made the Iraq War the deadliest conflict in history, in spite of being under the watchful eyes of the US military and the world's media.

After obtaining some of the study's data and details on methodology, Spagat published a peer-reviewed article in *Defense and Peace Economics* that detailed several steps where Burnham's data could have been faked or altered without notice. For one thing, Burnham's team published no information about the supervision of interviewers in Iraqi cities; there was therefore no way to verify whether someone actually traveled where they said they did, spoke to anyone, or verified deaths. Spagat found evidence of possible fabrication and wrote, for example, about interviews conducted in the region of Al-Tameem:

> Data are missing on the number of males and the number of females for all 40 households. This can be viewed as another quality control issue; someone should have spotted this deficiency and sent field workers back to this cluster to gather the missing data.[6]

In another cluster of interviews in the northern city of Nineveh, Spagat found that Burnham's data recorded 42 deaths, 35 of which are classified as violent. According to respondents, 18 people died by "air strike," 10 from "gunshot," 4 from "car bombs," and so on. But according to Spagat, none of these 18 deaths recorded as being due to an air strike were confirmed by an official certificate; in 7 cases, the interviewers "forgot" to, or simply did not, ask for one, and in 11 others they requested to see death certificates, but respondents could not produce any. Spagat concludes that various aspects of the data are consistent with the possibility of some fabrication. We are left to wonder how many other alleged "deaths" recorded in Burnham's study resulted from similar data issues, raising questions about the high death toll that was reported.

Spagat raises the possibility that the statistical anomalies in Burnham's study stem from poor training of interviewers, a broader problem with survey research when supervision is lax. For example, in order to save time (and money), or to avoid danger, fabrication is common enough that researchers have invented a term for it: in "curbstoning," interviewers, perhaps while sitting on the street curb instead of visiting interviewees, invent survey responses, either by imagining an interview completely, or duplicating responses from an actual interviewee. Researchers are especially worried about curbstoning in conflict zones. Several pollsters told me that they trust very little of the work both academics and governments conducted in the Middle East before 2012 or so.

Concerns have been raised about the potential for data fabrication at any stage in the survey process where there is insufficient supervision. For example, Michael Spagat has raised questions about a September 2007 opinion poll of 2,000 Iraqi citizens that involved twenty-two supervisors overseeing a large team of interviewers to conduct face-to-face surveys across Iraq.[7] According to a paper by Spagat, of these twenty-two supervisors, six provided data from 684 interviews that displayed "remarkable irregularities." Spagat cited as an example of this that, with respect to one question, every single respondent reported that they owned a short-wave radio—an unusually high percentage. But in a follow-up question, not a single person said they had listened to it; instead, the interviewers recorded that 472 Iraqis said that they "never" listened to their radio (and 212 people were recorded as "not eligible" for a response).[8]

Viewed alone, that single apparent irregularity might be explained as a simple data-entry or other error; interviewers are only human, and such things happen. However, according to Spagat's findings, the supervisors who recorded "normal" data reported a healthy mix of people who did not own a shortwave radio—and those who did said they had listened to their radios over the last day, week, or month. Spagat also found that the United States sponsored another poll in Iraq in 2008 in which precisely the same six supervisors—who were identified in each survey by a unique serial number—had generated dozens of other suspicious patterns.[9]

Spagat first became aware of the inconsistencies in these surveys in 2011 from Steve Koczela, a survey researcher who had worked on the US State Department's polling in Iraq. After leaving the department, Koczela retrieved data collected by US government contractors via academic survey archives held at the Roper Center (then at the University of Connecticut and now at Cornell) and a Freedom of Information Act request. Spagat and Koczela (who was not involved in publication of the results of his and Spagat's findings) were able to combine the raw data files for four surveys that the Broadcasting Board of Governors had commissioned with two other surveys that had been conducted by the University of Maryland's Program on International Policy Attitudes. According to Spagat, KA Research Limited, a Middle East–based company that worked with a US company called D3 Systems, had performed the fieldwork for all these polls.[10]

The information uncovered strongly suggested that some data had very likely been fabricated. In a 2011 paper, Spagat explored several different trends in the six aforementioned surveys of public opinion in Iraq.[11] According to Spagat's findings and the data files he published with them, the data exhibited clear patterns of fabrication, at the supervisor level. For example, in a December 2005 survey, none of 418 people "interviewed" by the six "focal supervisors" rated Turkey "very favorably." Given that

328 out of the 2,519 respondents for the other supervisors (roughly 13%) were so inclined, Spagat says, this result is highly unlikely. And in a September 2007 poll, the 684 respondents who were gathered by interviewers reporting to the suspect supervisors answered three separate questions with the exact same answers, indicating that they never use foreign satellite TV, international radio, or text messaging for information about current events. Yet more than a third of the respondents for the other supervisors chose different responses.[12]

Responses from the "same people" also seem suspect, as many "gave" answers to multiple questions that are inherently contradictory or reflections of attitudes that are implausibly held at the same time. At a minimum, the responses suggest that people were very confused by the questions. In other cases, this could be suggestive of fabrication. For example, take the following two questions from one survey Spagat analyzed:

1. "How important is it to you, personally, to stay informed about news and current events?"
2. "How interested are you, personally, to stay informed about current events in Iraq?"

Spagat found there was virtually no relationship between answers to these prompts among the "surveys" from interviewers reporting to the six focal supervisors. Read literally, this means it was just as likely that those Iraqis simultaneously valued and paid attention to news on current events as it was they said it was "important" to stay informed, but not "interesting," the latter certainly being a seemingly anomalous result. For the surveys within the other supervisors' remits, the answers to these two questions were much more strongly related.[13]

Spagat's findings of questionable data did not stop there. According to his analysis of separate surveys conducted by KA Research on behalf of the US State Department, interviewers reporting to the suspect supervisors all recorded that nobody they talked to selected three of five possible answers to questions about utility service—a nearly impossible pattern called "partial distribution." Unlike the interviews conducted by pollsters reporting to the other supervisors, everyone reported as having been surveyed by the interviewers reporting to the six focal supervisors said their service was "very good," "good," or they didn't know; in an April 2006 poll, the exact same number of people also said their electrical supply was "poor" or "very poor"; the same for their telephone service, traffic management, and garbage collection.[14]

Problems of data fabrication have surfaced in other surveys conducted on behalf of the US State Department. One former official at the State Department's Office of Opinion Research under the Bureau of Intelligence and Research (INR/OPN), which oversees the organizations for which these polls were done, said many employees turned a blind eye to the problems with the data from these surveys. Instead, they continued with business as usual. Some of the data were compiled in internal memos and executive briefings, perhaps even making their way to the president. And although the State Department still refuses to publicly acknowledge that much of their polling during the Iraq War was based on fraudulent interviews,[15] one official admitted knowing about the errors at the time, during a conference organized by the Washington Statistical Society (WSS) in December 2014.

According to recordings of the conference, David Nolle, who worked for the INR/OPN, told the WSS audience that there was "lots of data fabrication" in overseas opinion surveys, and explicitly conceded that Steve Koczela's work for the department brought "extreme" errors to their attention. He detailed a pattern of multiple companies across several countries providing fraudulent survey data to the US government, a symptom of "a culture" of bad survey research that posed "a major problem" to government intelligence collection. According to Nolle, after Koczela had left the State Department, he found evidence of fabrication in several surveys and directed an unnamed contractor to fire nineteen interviewers, two supervisors, and two coders, "all of whom were involved" with the scheme. The incident prompted OPN/INR to later institute quality control programs that they use to this day.

A CRISIS OF CONFIDENCE

These survey errors may sound far off and irrelevant to Americans. Most problem areas for international research are, by definition, a world away. But people should be concerned any time public opinion polls can be used to further an agenda or pollute the process of government representation.

And problems can be closer than they first appear. For example, ABC News and a group of international media partners hired D3 Systems to conduct a series of polls for a project on the brutality of postwar life in Iraq. It won the network two Emmy awards (the first ever to mention public opinion polls) and the prestigious "Policy Impact Award" of the AAPOR (American Association for Public Opinion Research) in 2010. The pollster for ABC News, Gary Langer, maintains that there was no fabrication in the data they received from the pollsters, insisting that the suspect patterns are not proof of fabrication. He has not released their data publicly for verification.[16] It is possible that they received clean data while the other clients did not, but that is hard to believe.

The problems in international surveys were also broader than one or two questions. Michael Robbins, the director of Arab Barometer, an academic project devoted to surveying Middle Eastern states, has alleged much more widespread contamination of international public opinion polling, particularly in countries that are not members of the Organisation for Economic Co-operation and Development (OECD, a committee of representatives from thirty-eight mostly western developed countries that publishes reports and issues rules to further economic growth). For example, he found that roughly half of all interviews conducted in Lebanon for a Pew Research Center survey in 2013 were potentially fabricated.[17] These interviews exceeded the threshold of a statistical test that he and a colleague developed called "percent match" measuring the percentage of responses given by one interviewee that are identical to another person's. If one entry is an 85% match to another, according to their test, there is a significant risk that the entries are duplications or fabrications.

Robbins and his coauthor, Noble Kuriakose, published an application of their test in the *Statistical Journal* of the International Association for Official Statistics in early 2016. They started by collecting 1,008 national surveys from 154 countries that included 1.2 million interviews in total. All but a few of the polls surveyed more than 1,000 people, each asking them over 75 questions.

For each survey, Robbins and Kuriakose evaluated the extent to which each respondent's answers "matched" the answers from another respondent. If two people gave perfectly matched answers to every question, the likelihood for fraud was very high. After running their analysis, Robbins and Kuriakose found that the vast majority of surveys from OECD countries contained very few high-probability duplicates; 36% contained no potential duplicate cases at all, and in another 47% of polls the duplicates amounted to less than 5% of the sample. These levels of fabrication would be too small to meaningfully alter the results from most polls. Moreover, the authors found that 96% of polls collected in these countries contained almost no (<5%) potentially duplicated data whatsoever.

However, Robbins and Kuriakose wrote that nearly one out of every five of the 1,008 polls from non-OECD countries contained near-duplicates amounting to 5% or more of the people sampled in that survey (e.g., 50 potential duplicates in a 1,000-person poll). One in every ten polls contained near-duplicates amounting to more than 10% of interviewees. In these circumstances, the authors alleged, it was highly likely (though not guaranteed) that something was wrong with the data.

These results ought to have blown the lid off the fabrication crisis in international polling. However, Robbins and Kuriakose ran into a problem: the Pew Research Center, one of the biggest and most reputable polling firms, opposed their test. Pew's methods team claimed the algorithm can mistakenly flag as potential duplicates members of homogenous groups—such as religious minorities or ethnic enclaves—who naturally give similar answers to many questions. It is also not sensible to apply the test to short polls with few answer options on each question, as just by random chance, interviews will receive suspect scores. Pew has disavowed the test, saying this and other holes in the test make it unreliable in too many circumstances.

Pew's methodological critiques were valid, but would have mostly impacted outlier cases of data fabrication. In fact, Robbins and Kuriakose conceded most of these points in their academic article on the algorithm. Robbins rightly argues that "no statistical test is applicable in every circumstance" but that, with the right poll, percent match can be useful as a guide. The test does not detect outright fraud, but only tells you whether something "merits additional investigation." The president of the Pew Research Center, Michael Dimock, also wrote later that "data quality deserves an honest discussion,"[18] so the organization seemed to be rightly concerned about the issue anyway. Perhaps they just wanted the conversation to unfold on their own terms. Further studies have found the "percent match" metric to be one of the best predictors of faulty data.[19] It is plausible that the Pew Research Center uses an adapted version in their own work today.

The good news is that fabrication has nearly become a thing of the past. Michael Robbins, Steve Koczela, the State Department's Office of Opinion Research, and many other researchers have developed protocols and computer programs to detect fabrication and prevent poisoning the well of research. Face-to-face interviewers are now required to submit responses to questions on smartphones, tablets, or laptops in real time. This "computer-assisted personal interviewing" (CAPI) also allows managers to remotely record audio, GPS location data, and pictures of surroundings to ensure that interviewers actually conducted the surveys they say they did. Statistical algorithms such as percent match can also help detect potential instances of fraud before a survey is released to the public.

RAISING THE PUBLIC PULSE

Potential data fabrication is not the only way pollsters can act nefariously. Additional patterns of wrongdoing show how engaging in bad-faith research and mistakes of judgment can contaminate the information society receives from the pollsters. Luckily, the instances are rare. But they must nevertheless be rooted out.

Examples of so-called push polling, where campaign workers or consultants pretend to be pollsters in order to spread negative stories or hurt a candidate's ratings, were widespread enough in the 2008 election that the Comedy Central show *The Colbert Report* based a minute-long sketch on them. In the clip, Stephen Colbert is filmed finishing a faux push poll for Republican primary candidate Mike Huckabee. "Do you strongly agree, strongly disagree, or have no opinion about the following statement: 'I would continue to support Senator McCain for president if I learned he had fathered an illegitimate Asian baby'?" he asks a faux respondent over an old touch-tone phone. "How about this: An illegitimate, pirate baby? . . . What about a legitimate Nazi baby?" Colbert finishes the call by asking, "That would be bad, wouldn't it? Okay, I gotta go, vote your conscience, bye-bye!"[20] Turning back to the audience, he remarks: "Sorry, I was just finishing up some push polling for my friend Mike Huckabee."[21]

Though campaigns seldom resort to such tricks, the sketch was based in reality. John McCain's earlier 2000 campaign for the Republican nomination for president was dogged by rumors that were factually baseless but politically dangerous. He had fathered a "Negro child" with a woman he was not married to, fliers left on cars outside a candidates' debate in Columbia, South Carolina, alleged. Rumors also circulated that his wife, Cindy, was addicted to prescription painkillers; that John cheated on

Cindy with prostitutes; some called him the "Fag" candidate. The precise source of these particular lies was never found.[22]

Later, according to *Vanity Fair* reporter Richard Gooding, several figures who supported Bush's campaign admitted to spreading the lies via push polling.[23] If you were in South Carolina in 2000, you may have answered your phone and had someone try using thinly veiled questions about obvious falsehoods or slanted facts. A conversation might go like this:

INTERVIEWER: Hi, may I speak to John Deer?

DEER: Yes, this is John.

INTERVIEWER: Hi, I'm a pollster with the Independent Group
    for Political Citizens, and I'm calling to ask a few questions
    about who you're voting for. In the upcoming race between
    John McCain and George Bush, who would you vote for?

DEER: Yeah, uh, I think I'll vote for McCain.

INTERVIEWER: Would you still vote for McCain if you knew he
    had sex with prostitutes and gave his wife venereal disease?

DEER: Yeah, that doesn't really bother me.

INTERVIEWER: Well, would you vote for McCain if you knew he
    ran over his ex-wife with his car?

. . . And so on.

IN 2004, THE AMERICAN RESEARCH GROUP (ARG), a polling firm from New Hampshire, told Gooding that the firm's interviewers in South Carolina in 2000 were interviewing people who would say they had just received a push poll from someone else. According to ARG, the push pollsters made life difficult for legitimate firms because people were "afraid that as soon as they say who they're for, they're gonna get whacked." This could decrease their willingness to answer the phone, or to make them suspect that legitimate-seeming interviews might become push polls at any point.[24]

Sometimes, pollsters also appear to alter the methods or data of their polls ad hoc, with the effect of bringing them in line with estimates from other firms. In 2012, Public Policy Polling (PPP), a company based in North Carolina that conducts surveys all over the country and serves a mostly left-leaning client base, admitted to randomly deleting respondents in their data to bring the remaining respondents into "target ranges" for race, gender, and age based on prior exit polls and census data, projecting the electorate's racial composition by using respondents' 2008 candidate preferences. "On every day of PPP's tracking poll," Nate Cohn, who now runs polls for the *New York Times*, wrote in 2012, "PPP's survey produced a result closer to the average of polls than they would have if they consistently used the composition of the electorate from their final poll." Though it's impossible to prove, Cohn wondered whether the adjustments could have been used to bring the poll's estimates closer in line with previous polls or the consensus of other pollsters—a fact that is exceedingly troubling in an environment where pollsters and their methods are not heavily regulated by any oversight organization. Cohn reported that PPP's director, Tom Jensen, insisted its polling was accurate, their clients were satisfied, and "the only thing we're trying to accomplish when weighting our polls is to accurately tell people what would happen if the election was today." As Cohn put it, "the problem is that it's very difficult to distinguish these statements from weighting toward a desired result," something Cohn acknowledged it was impossible to prove—but troubling because it was "totally possible."[25]

Public Policy Polling is hardly the only public polling company that has been scrutinized for allegedly tweaking their methodology to stay close to polling averages. Take the case of the right-leaning pollster Rasmussen Reports, which puzzlingly deleted a poll of the 2014 Kansas Senate race from its website shortly after it was released. At the time, political blogger Harry Enten and FiveThirtyEight's Nate Silver wondered whether the firm did so because they "got cold feet" when CNN and Fox News published polls with which Rasmussen's was far out of line. Confronted by Enten, a representative for the firm said the numbers were actually deleted because they were "basically raw data"—unpublished numbers that hadn't been weighted or checked for errors—that had been published inadvertently. They promised to release the poll once the processing errors were fixed. But days passed without corrected data materializing. When Enten and Silver reached them again, Rasmussen said they "realized that an error was made in the programming of the survey that may have skewed the data" and would be releasing results from a new poll later on. Rasmussen never publicly specified what the error was, but it did follow through on its promise to release another poll a few weeks later. The final result was much closer to the numbers released by other pollsters.[26]

On another occasion, John Anzalone, who conducts polls for Democratic candidates, admitted on Twitter that when his firm conducts a poll they believe too far away from the average—an outlier—they "redo the poll at [their] expense. Period."[27]

Increasingly, public pollsters are willing to skew their results to cater to one side of the aisle or the other. In the past, when an organization published routinely biased numbers and didn't act transparently or with methodological rigor, they would be at high risk of losing clients and possibly be sanctioned by the AAPOR. But in our modern age of echo chambers and polarized media outlets, even those pollsters who peddle conspiracy theories or manipulate data to suit their purposes can receive press coverage and clients who share their ideological goals.

Rasmussen Reports routinely releases estimates that are biased toward Republican candidates—both before they win and after. Rasmussen's polls almost always overestimated the share of Americans who approved of Donald Trump's job as president, for example, often with an average bias greater than five percentage points. Individual polls were frequently even more out of whack. When questioned, Rasmussen Reports said that other pollsters simply had an anti-Trump bias that they were adjusting for.[28]

Other pollsters also show signs of deviation that cannot be due to standard methodological choices alone. Andrew Gelman, a Columbia University statistician and political scientist with whom I worked on a pre-election presidential forecast in 2020 for *The Economist*, posted a study that October that shows a small, opaque pollster called the Trafalgar Group had the most reliably Republican bias of any firm we included in our model.[29]

Before the election, the firm's owner, Robert Cahaly, attested that the bias was due to their black-box correction for people's tendency to lie about supporting Donald Trump (pollsters and political psychologists have found no evidence for this pattern). "We live in a country where people will lie to their accountant, they'll lie to their doctor, they'll lie to their priest," Cahaly told *Politico* before the election. "And we're supposed to believe they shed all of that when they get on the telephone with a stranger and become Honest Abe? . . . There's a lot of hidden Trump votes out there. Will Biden win the popular vote? Probably. I'm not even debating that. But I think Trump is likely to have an Electoral College victory."[30]

Cahaly spent the final weeks making the rounds on conservative media outlets. The *Wall Street Journal* did a profile on him. Appearing with his signature bow tie, goatee, and Southern accent on Fox News' *Sunday Morning Futures* with Maria Bartiromo, the popular right-leaning television host, Cahaly proclaimed that traditional polls were outdated and that pollsters "haven't learned any lessons" since 2016. "You're going to be shocked," he said.[31] On the night before the election, Cahaly predicted that Donald Trump would win most of the states he won in 2016, plus Arizona. He was wrong about five states, whereas the polling averages missed in only two.

THE BABY IN THE BATHWATER

While good polling is an expression of public opinion and a force for good in capturing the will of the demos, hope and optimism will not keep unreliable or politically motivated pollsters at bay. To avoid contaminating the information ecosystem, pollsters must enforce a culture of science and transparency in order to hold bad actors to account. Journalists and leaders have to ignore bad polls, even when it is inconvenient for them, and be honest about the scientific process that generated the data. Consumers of polls need to internalize that they are scientific, yes, but not surgically precise.

The mirror that is the public opinion poll is not just cracked; there are blemishes and other imperfections that might render reflections imprecise, too. The process of squinting past these obstacles strains our attention and muddies the peripheral context of our reality. But although the mirror does not offer up a perfect reflection, one blemish does not render the mirror useless. One or two bad polls do not make the hundreds of others any less useful. Poll-readers must be vigilant to separate the good from the bad—to find the right angle to stare into the mirror, rather than throwing it to the floor.

5

AMERICA IN AGGREGATE

Critical thinking is an active and ongoing process. It requires that we all think like Bayesians, updating our knowledge as new information comes in.

—DANIEL LEVITIN, *A FIELD GUIDE TO LIES*, 2016

I t is neither new nor surprising that media outlets today pay so much attention to pre-election polling and election forecasts. Ever since the first straw polls were collected, newspapers clamored to publish the results. Soothsaying sells—big-time. One analysis of web traffic during the 2016 presidential election campaign found that cable news outlets mentioned election predictions around sixteen times per day.[1] Before an election, predictions are the biggest story of the year.

Paradoxically, the enormous attention paid to election polls and forecasts may have left the public utterly confused about what it is polls do, and how predictions are really made. Do polls predict outcomes? Well, kind of. But what about some outlet's so-called polling averages?

Or the "probabilistic forecasts"? Are those polls too? If not, what is the difference?

POLLING THE POLLSTERS

Pollsters are fond of saying that their polls only represent "snapshots in time"—that their data only show the distribution of opinions today and cannot foresee what might happen in the coming days, weeks, or months. This is true, but it is more excuse than anything else. The popularity of the phrase today likely grew out of the industry's poorly timed and errant forecasts of elections such as the 1948 presidential contest, when opinions shifted after final polls were taken.

If you want a prediction, you should not go directly to a pollster. They are likely to give you all the nuance and uncertainty that are inherent in their data—not the stuff that most journalists are looking to hand off to their editors, who want attention-grabbing, confident predictions. For your own polling oracle, you will have to go to a television pundit or a prognosticator. Sure, they are liable to simply look at the data from pollsters and strip out the nuance, but now you will have your prediction. But what do you do if different polls give different pictures of the race?

One answer is to average them together. In October 1992, a senior political analyst for CNN named William Schneider reported his analysis of a "poll of polls" concept for combining the results of different surveys. He took a poll of polls, or "polling average" in his words, because all polls are "subject to error" and he wanted to "see how much consistency there is across all of the polls."[2]

The concept of a "poll of polls" was not new in political journalism, though it may still have been poorly understood. The British newspaper *The Sunday Times* began publishing the first widespread "poll of polls" in the 1970s. By 1992, *The Economist* was publishing its own meta-polls of US elections, which it highlighted on a weekly basis during the fall presidential campaign. A few domestic American outlets also began mentioning their own averages, but they lacked the notoriety and frequency of the CNN product.[3]

Back then, polls of polls were primitive, opaque, and rather crude. The methods used to calculate them were not typically explained to readers, and many news outlets did not even explain what polls they consisted of. It would have been impossible to know if a publisher was thumbing the scale. But the polls of polls, or polling averages as they're more commonly called today, do usually provide better estimates of pre-election opinion than any one poll ever would. Their secret weapon is their ability to combat that age-old problem of sampling error.

Imagine for a moment that you are picking colored marbles out of a large sack. Inside, you are told, there are 50% blue marbles and 50% yellow. You stick your hand in, eyes closed, and withdraw one marble at random. It's yellow. You sample again—blue. Two more times you repeat the drawing, and each time you pull out a blue marble. You might now be tempted to believe this means that the bag consists overwhelmingly of blue marbles, but in fact, your outcome is not so unlikely with a 50-50 sack. Given that the probability of each draw coming up either blue or yellow is 50%, there is roughly a 13% chance that you will select three of the same color in a row.

But you really want to know if the bag is a fair bag! So you draw six more marbles, for a total of ten. This time, the marbles come up blue, then yellow, then yellow again, then blue, yellow, and yellow. After ten draws you have the following sample of marbles:

Y B B B B Y Y B Y Y

You have selected five blue marbles and five yellow: precisely 50% for each. You could continue your experiment, but you stop there—you are satisfied that the bag has equal shares of both colors.

Now imagine you have multiple sacks that each need to be counted for fairness. You could tally all the colors in each, or you could repeat the sampling process and record the results. But in three successive bags you observe an apparent bias toward blue, then yellow, then blue marbles. What gives? Take yourself out of the experiment now. Since you and I know the experiment has been set up so that the sacks of marbles are actually equal in composition of yellow and blue marbles, we know your imaginary self has just observed sampling error at work.

Statistically, the theory of sampling error states that when drawing a few items from a larger set, you are not guaranteed to get a representative sample. But your odds of doing so increase as you select more marbles. Perhaps, next time, withdraw twenty—or 200—from the sack instead of just ten. This is called the law of large numbers; the more times you conduct an experiment, the closer the average result will be to the expected value of the exercise.

Although people are not marbles in a sack, polls work in a similar fashion to our example. Any individual survey—say, of 1,000 people out of a population of 300 million—has a chance of drawing a biased sample, even if all of its other methods are perfectly designed. This is one reason why CNN's Bill Schneider says that "no poll is authoritative"; no matter how it's designed or how many people it samples, there is always a chance that one single poll could miss the precise outcome of an election. But what if you average them together?

In 2005, a political scientist named Charles Franklin had a similar idea to Schneider's. Franklin, an Alabamian living in the Midwest, fits the stereotype of a nerdy professor (though by his own description, he is more of a "geek"—whatever the difference): he has close-cropped hair, wears wire-framed glasses, and shares pictures online of his sophisticated computer setup for analyzing polling data in his home office.

To his fellow political science geeks, Franklin has a very impressive résumé. In school, his thesis was advised by John Jackson, a notable social science statistician. Franklin wrote about how survey respondents would frequently change their stated party affiliation over time—a big challenge to the conventional wisdom among political scientists at the time. He was also a research assistant for Angus Campbell, Philip Converse, and Warren Miller at the University of Michigan, three of the pioneers of academic survey analysis and voter behavior. Today he is professor of law and public policy at Marquette University, where he is the director of its Law School Poll.

After Hurricane Katrina decimated New Orleans in 2005, Franklin was curious about whether George W. Bush's poor handling of the crisis was hurting his approval ratings. But he was confronted by the same problems that Bill Schneider had attempted to solve with his network's poll of polls: How do you know which number is right? If you throw every number in a hat, what is the best method for summarizing them all?

Franklin's solution was similar to Schneider's, but more technically sophisticated. He would compute a "trend line" by gathering data from individual approval rating polls and applying statistical techniques called "smoothing" and "aggregation." In contrast with the most common technique of aggregation, which is to take an average of the results from polls that are conducted in a certain period—maybe the last week or so—and update it over time, Franklin calculated an equation for a line through each point that minimized the distance between the poll's estimate and the line. The equation for this line could change over time, allowing for a smooth transition between estimates on one day and estimates a week from then.

On September 9, 2005, Franklin published his first estimates of Bush's approval rating on his blog *Political Arithmetik* (the name is a reference to a pamphlet published by British economist Sir William Petty in 1690). His novel polling aggregate showed a steep decline for the president, from roughly a 50% approval rating in February to a 44% rating in September. The post was his first aggregate of several polls and the first graph of a president's job approval average to be widely cited across the web. Before 2005, graphic displays of very crude moving averages of election polls were available online, but nothing similar existed for approval ratings, and other election averages were not as methodologically advanced as Franklin's. Though he does not get much credit for it, Franklin was one of the founders of modern methods for polling aggregation.[4]

THE MYSTERY POLLSTER

In 2006, Charles Franklin walked into a (now-closed) Mediterranean restaurant on Monroe Street in Madison, Wisconsin—where he had been a professor since 1992—to have lunch with Mark Blumenthal, another big figure in the world of polling bloggers. Blumenthal had been posting his own analyses of election polls online under the (de-anonymized) pseudonym "Mystery Pollster" since September 2004. "We recognized each other quickly," Franklin says, "because we were the only two nerds there." They parted ways after the lunch—Blumenthal had other business in town—but would soon be in touch again.

Blumenthal's own blog was less technical than Franklin's, targeted more toward Washington insiders and media elites than academics. He was not writing as a scientist of the data, but rather claimed to be a "pundit about polling." He drew on his experience conducting polls for clients, his interest in politics, and connections to the goings-on in Washington. Blumenthal's posts were more closely tied to the daily humdrum of new polling releases and the conversations about data that were swirling inside the Beltway. Chuck Todd, now the host of NBC's *Meet the Press* and then the editor of The Hotline (a popular daily politics blog published by a media and government services company called National Journal), had frequent exchanges with Blumenthal about the polls and his writing. On some occasions, he would raise objections to Mark's points, as in an email exchange in December 2005 in which he "chided" Blumenthal for focusing on only one question in a new poll Todd's outlet had sponsored. Other times, he recommended the Mystery Pollster to his audience. One day early on in the blog's history, political commentator Michael "Mickey" Kaus linked to Blumenthal's site, and 7,000 readers clicked through—a lot for a guy just starting out in the business.[5]

But Blumenthal, by his own admission, did not have any grand plans for his up-and-coming blog. He commanded the attention of several powerful insiders in Washington, but few outlets expressed interest in bringing his blog onto their domain, or adding him onto their payroll. That all changed when Douglas Rivers, a Stanford political science professor and then the CEO of an online polling firm called Polimetrix, expressed interest in hosting both Blumenthal's posts and Franklin's charts online at Pollster.com, which he had bought many years earlier and was "looking for something to do with." By Blumenthal's account, the deal was a long way from being imminently or obviously profitable, but they all decided to put in the effort and "see what happened." Rivers hired a few developers to make a site that hosted Franklin's trend-analysis charts of approval rating, election, and other polling, and hired Blumenthal to provide blog posts. Pollster.com, under the new sponsorship of Polimetrix, went online in September 2006.

Nerds loved the site. The trio's decision to chart a polling average through individual points for each poll (as Franklin had pioneered on his blog) was a revolutionary development in polling analysis. Their estimates of both the "true" aggregate state of public opinion and the uncertainty in their calculations was the most sophisticated popular analysis of polls available at the time. Other journalists chose to ignore results from certain firms, or picked the high and low outliers to emphasize movement that probably wasn't real. Blumenthal and Franklin's thinking was different. "In a world where there is a variety of polls and they use different methodologies with variations in questions and are done across different survey organizations," Franklin told me, "we thought it was important for people to see the mean and variation all in one place instead of having to read all the different articles about the same topic."

From the business side, however, things at Pollster.com were not looking good. "Nobody in the world [wanted] to invest in an advertiser-supported niche website," Blumenthal recalled. The primary issue was that the site didn't generate enough traffic to translate into meaningful revenue. Only during election seasons did it get enough hits to even come close to paying for the salaries of its staff, web hosting, and website upkeep. For the other twenty-two months out of every two years, traffic was too low to sustain the business. Rivers's investment was not going to be enough in the long term, and existing partnerships did not provide significant salary support. They had Slate.com, the popular political blog, pay a modest fee to access the crew's data. And the National Journal had also provided office space in the Watergate complex for Mark and two other employees, in exchange for a frequent column from Blumenthal and the ability to sell ads on the Pollster.com domain.[6]

These deals worked for a time, but by 2008 the reality of the site's fiscal issues had become clear. Rivers had spent more than he had originally envisioned for the moderate success they had achieved so far. "We had three goals for Pollster when we started," Blumenthal said. "We wanted to do a pro-bono project for the survey research field . . . and collect everything . . . if for no other reason than to know which pollster was right after the election." At the time, nobody else was doing that work well. They also wanted to build an audience, and a brand. They succeeded at that. "And we had the goal of making money on it. We did two out of three," Blumenthal said. "We struggled to find some kind of business model that would work."

By the summer of 2010, the Pollster team was running on fumes. They had "exhausted" (Blumenthal's word) the goodwill of its sponsors and partners, and advertising revenue had plummeted as a result of the 2007–8 global financial crisis. Rivers was ready to redirect his focus to another project. The time was right for a buyout, and *Huffington Post* had submitted an offer. In exchange for office space, much-needed web development expertise, and reasonable salaries, Blumenthal and a few data-crunchers would migrate their content and rebrand Pollster.com under the *Huffington Post* banner. The deal also solved the primary weakness in the original trio's business model: in election years, *Huffington Post* Pollster would make a load of cash to share across the organization; in off years, the team's salaries would be funded by profits made elsewhere.

Over the next two years, the team put together the new *Huffington Post* Pollster.com. It had a slick new look and a revised polling database. It went live on September 29, 2010, and the benefits of the deal were immediately clear; whereas the team's posts would normally reach 7,000–8,000 people in a week, the *Huffington* homepage was sending tens of thousands of clicks to Mark's articles by the hour. The first piece he published was at four o'clock on a Friday, ordinarily a bad time to publish news, as most people have tuned out for the week. It got 80,000 views by eight o'clock that night.

The period from 2010 to 2015 was the heyday for *Huffington Post* Pollster. The homepage was one of the most visited websites on the internet, giving Blumenthal and his team direct access to hundreds of thousands of readers at the click of a button. In 2012, the crew hired a political scientist and statistician named Simon Jackman to build a top-of-the-line election prediction model. It correctly predicted the result of the presidential election, and as a bonus, introduced millions of readers to the team's original ideas of the wisdom of aggregation and the importance of showing uncertainty in polling averages.

But in 2015, Blumenthal left *Huffington Post* for good. He was burned out and ready for something new, so he moved back into private polling and took a job at an online firm called SurveyMonkey, which provides a platform for people to conduct polls of their friends, organization, or company via email. He left Pollster in the capable hands of Ariel Edwards-Levy, a reporter who is still at *Huffington Post*, and Natalie Jackson, a pollster who designed another election model for the company in 2016 and went back into private (and, later, public) polling in 2017.

Blumenthal got out at a favorable time. Despite Pollster's apparent successes after 2010—receiving stratospheric election-year traffic and pushing an ideological shift in the way journalists and the public interpret polling data—by the middle of the 2010s the site was on its last legs. Algorithmic news feeds at social media companies, especially Facebook, had created a new method by which people read news: instead of turning to aggregation websites, they just read what their friends shared. The *Huffington Post*'s ad revenue fell precipitously. In 2011, AOL had bought the outlet for $315 million; by 2019, it was laying off staff and AOL was looking for a buyer.

A RANDOM WALK DOWN MAIN STREET

The rise of polling aggregation websites such as Pollster.com created a better way for journalists to cover political polling. A good model, like Charles Franklin's, is necessary to communicate the findings from an array of polls. An election forecast can be thought of as a similar itera-tion: whereas aggregators answer the question of who is leading in the polls today, forecasters tell you how likely that is to change by Election Day. But, importantly, forecasts and polls are not one and the same. Polls, their creators stress, cannot tell you anything about what might happen in the future. The forecasters have to bring in their own analysis to create such predictions.

One reason for Pollster's mixed success was the incredible popularity of Nate Silver, a rival polling aggregator and election forecaster. Silver not only took the polls and averaged them together, but he created probabilis-tic models to answer the second-order question of how safe a candidate's lead was. In other words, he did not just want to know how big a lead a candidate had *today*, but whether the typical range of movement in poll-ing aggregates for previous elections was large enough that the candidates currently trailing in the polls could conceivably dethrone the leader. If Franklin and Blumenthal brought aggregation to the mainstream, Sil-ver's chief contribution to the field of political statistics was in quantify-ing the uncertainty of the future.

The prediction model that Silver created in the spring of 2008 is the product of this insight. On February 26, he laid out a first draft of his methodology in a blog post: "right now there are three recent Wiscon-sin polls that show Obama beating McCain by an average of 4 points," he wrote. "How does this translate in terms of the general election, which is still more than 250 days away? Is Obama a massive favorite over McCain—or is it closer to a toss-up?"[7]

Deriving the answer requires doing a little bit of statistics, but not much more than a pollster would have done. You can do the entire process with one spreadsheet in Microsoft Excel. The first step is to collect as many polls as you can in each state and average the results. In the first of Silver's models, this average was a crude moving average in each state. Later, he would go on to give more weight to polls that were conducted more recently, using something called an "exponentially weighted moving average," and to give more weight to pollsters who were more accurate in the past—what he called a "reliability rating." This was a key insight that set him apart from other aggregators such as Pollster and RealClear-Politics that give essentially the same weight to all polls.

The second step involves predicting what the polls would say in a state that does not have any data yet. For the Democratic primary, Silver matched up demographic data and past election results to predict the polling averages in states where he had enough data, then made projections for states that didn't yet have polls. In essence, he was creating polls in unpolled states.

So far, this is all relatively easy to do. The final step in the forecast, however, is a little tricky. The polling average alone in each state does not tell you much if you're asking questions about probability. You have to go beyond the polls as they are, and answer the question of what will happen if they are wrong. Silver did this using a technique called the Monte Carlo method, which was developed in the 1940s and involves repeatedly generating a randomly distributed number to vary some quantity of interest, allowing you to make inferences under conditions of uncertainty. In Silver's case, the first version of his model ran 5,000 Monte Carlo simulations to see what would happen if polls were uniformly biased toward Obama or McCain, based on how wrong they had been in the past.

This process yields 5,000 different potential maps of the election, each exploring a different scenario. What if Obama beats his polls everywhere and wins the popular vote by 10 points? What if he loses ground over the election? What if he beats his polls in Florida, but they're relatively accurate everywhere else? And so on. If you want to express these potential outcomes probabilistically, you simply count up the simulations in which Obama wins the election and divide by the total number of simulations. In the beta version of his model, Silver counted 3,210 simulations in which Obama won the Electoral College, and 1,790 where McCain won. That worked out to a probability of 64.2% that Obama would win. When he updated the model to account for pollster reliability and accuracy, on March 6, Obama's win probability had "dropped" to 63.9%. (The dip was meaningless, statistically speaking.)

Silver was also curious if Obama's competitor, Hillary Clinton, would do any better versus McCain. So he also ran 5,000 simulations using polls that asked how people would vote if she won the primary. Because her poll numbers in key states were worse than Obama's, Silver calculated just a 43.9% chance of Clinton winning. "A Hillary Nomination gives too many States away," a commenter named "Lefty Coaster" replied to Silver's post. In another post, "Serrano" (a riff on Silver's own username, "Poblano") wrote that the chart showing Clinton lagging behind Obama in electoral votes was "very Stark!!!" Redvolution, another commenter, asked if Silver had tried sending the analysis to the Obama campaign. "The Superdelegates need to see this." Another said, "You just made Chuck Todd your bitch. And I like Chuck Todd."

The morning after this post, a little after 8:00 AM on March 7, 2008, Silver purchased the domain name www.FiveThirtyEight.com to host an updated version of his projections.[8] Over the next two months, he posted updates about polls and the primary every day, and introduced an array of methodological tweaks to his model, including weighting the polling averages by sample size and adding more error in the simulations to account for the chance that all the polls from a given pollster could be off due to methodological error. He also added new variables to the regression to predict what polls would say in states that had none. Later, he added a "trend adjustment" to account for uniform national movement in the electoral environment over the course of the campaign, and made educated guesses about which candidate undecided voters would break for.

After the election, Silver claimed victory. His projections were on the right side of 50–50 in every state except Indiana. He appeared on cable news shows on MSNBC, CNN, and Fox News, and on the popular *Colbert Report*. His career was just beginning, but he had already changed political coverage forever. Silver quit his day job—running sports statistics for a company called Baseball Prospectus—and switched to election forecasting and political blogging full-time.

SOME MODELS ARE USEFUL

Nate Silver's 2008 election forecasting model was the first of its kind to make its way into political journalism. His embrace of probabilistic statistics and sophisticated polling aggregation has dramatically improved the way journalists cover election polls and the horse race. Journalists today focus much less than they used to on writing headlines about outlier polls, or blowing insignificant changes in one pollster's week-to-week numbers way out of proportion (although they still do this). Informed readers instead turn to RealClearPolitics and Pollster to know who's ahead, and to FiveThirtyEight to know whether they'll win.

Other media organizations could not ignore the attention that Silver and his polling model were getting. Having contracted Simon Jackman to produce their election model in 2012, in 2016 the *Huffington Post*'s Pollster team sought to produce a competing election model in-house. Natalie Jackson, a political scientist whom Mark Blumenthal had hired in 2014 and who had previously worked for Marist College conducting the polls for NBC News and the *Wall Street Journal*, was its chief architect.

Like all election models, Jackson's relied on the polls. Specifically, it used a modified version of the polling aggregation model that Charles Franklin had worked on years earlier. But her model was different from Silver's in two major ways. First, it varied in how it dealt with the polling data. Jackson's model did not adjust polling averages to take pollsters' record of accuracy into account, as Silver's did. It also did not include data from every single pollster; only the shops that disclosed a reasonable amount of technical information about their polls were included. In the team's collective mind, this helped separate the wheat from the chaff. Given the complexity of creating a good poll, this is a defensible position.

Second, Jackson made a consequential mistake elsewhere when setting up how her model dealt with uncertainty. She stuck "too close" to the data, in her words, and created a purely poll-driven model that did not simulate the chance that polls could be significantly and uniformly biased toward either candidate. "When it came to inserting extra uncertainty, I would go back and forth quite a bit," Jackson said in a 2021 interview. She and her software developer colleague ended up putting their trust in the data for what it was, only gaming out scenarios where polls were off inside their standard margin of error.[9] The model did not consider the eventuality that Donald Trump's voters would be significantly more likely than Hillary Clinton's to ignore pollsters' calls.

With the benefit of hindsight, this was an obvious mistake, Jackson says. But because she was making decisions in what she described as an environment of isolation, resource scarcity, and pressure from higher-ups to produce a forecast as soon as possible (one superior remarked that even a basic spreadsheet of polls would get enough clicks to satisfy them, according to Jackson), she did not see the misstep ahead of time. She maintains that she made the correct decision for the information and resources she had at her disposal. "What I was thinking about was that in the primaries and throughout 2015," Jackson told me, "everybody was like 'There's no way, there's no way, Trump can't do this.' And I'm sitting here staring at polling data that says 'Yes Trump is doing this.'" The primacy of polling over punditry in the Republican primary gave her a false sense of certainty that they would be accurate in November. To her credit, the polling averages in 2008 and 2012 were also abnormally accurate.

With that limited view of electoral history, and no staff to build out a more historical database, there was little reason to think that the polls in aggregate would wind up being as wrong as they were. Indeed, on November 8, 2016, a staffer at *Huffington Post*'s Washington, DC, bureau walked into their offices a block away from the White House with a bottle of champagne. They placed it at the back of the refrigerator in the kitchen around the corner from Natalie Jackson's desk. If everything went according to plan—Jackson's plan—they would pop the cork around 9 PM and declare an early victory, both for the forecast and for the staff's overwhelming favorite, Hillary Clinton.

Jackson spent the day conducting the usual business of a poll-informed political journalist. She cautioned against reading too much into early exit polls, which had led the media astray in 2004, and did a few passes over the model to determine how they'd know who was ahead, and when. But by 5:00 she was out of things to do. She went for a run around the National Mall, three blocks away, and thought to herself, "This is either going to be a really good night, or the worst moment of my career." Her colleagues had relied on her to tell them, with data, that Donald Trump had a very small chance of winning the election. What would happen if she were wrong?

Around 9 PM Eastern time, after it was clear Clinton would lose Florida, results from the Midwest started to trickle in. The data were disastrous for Democrats; some rural counties that had voted for Barack Obama over Mitt Romney by seven percentage points were going to Trump by twenty. The writing was on the wall. Jackson was trying to convince herself that it could still be okay, that her model—which gave Clinton a 98% chance of winning the election—would turn out okay.

By 9:30, she gave up. She sent an instant message to everyone in the newsroom saying, "I'm sorry, but we need to prepare for this going to

Trump." Jackson said she heard an audible gasp from her colleagues. She started crying, working through tears for the next five hours.

The champagne bottle in the fridge, once a symbol of the team's high expectation for Clinton (and Jackson), went unopened. Some members of the staff opted for harder stuff instead. Natalie called an Uber to take her back to her hotel in the Foggy Bottom neighborhood of DC around 2:45 AM. She did a radio interview at 3:15, crawled into bed, and sank into the night.

NATALIE JACKSON IS CALM when talking about the election now, years after her highly public miss led to months of online harassment and a career change (although she's back to producing polls again, now for a nonprofit think tank in DC). "Often in life those horrible, awful times on multiple dimensions are what you learn the most from," she told me. "Everybody has their bad patches, and it's what you do with it that matters."

But methodological mistakes matter, too. Although the race was close in the end, and the polls showed it, the forecasters who stuck too close to the data were blamed for misleading people about Clinton's chances. (Jackson was not the only one to give Clinton 98% chance of victory; a neuroscientist at Princeton University named Samuel Wang also ran a forecasting website that gave Clinton odds that were too high.) In his 2018 book *A Higher Loyalty*, former FBI director James Comey wrote that polls and forecasters led him to believe that he was "making decisions in an environment where Hillary Clinton was sure to be the next president." In such an environment, he claims he thought it was his duty to break with government norms and announce the continuation of a long-running investigation into her use of a private email server eleven days before the election—a move that may have sunk her candidacy.[10]

In comparison, Nate Silver's forecast gave Trump a 29% chance of winning in 2016—higher than Jackson's 2% or the *New York Times*'s 15%.

The nearly one-in-three shot implied that even a slightly larger than average polling error could be enough for him to overcome his apparent deficit. Of course, people are still liable to round a 30% probability closer to zero in their head. Forecasting's critics have to ask themselves whether they want to go back to the pre-Pollster, pre-Silver age when television pundits could choose whatever poll they wanted to make their point, without the accountability that a well-produced aggregate provides. In his 2005 book *Expert Political Judgment*, psychologist Philip Tetlock analyzed 82,000 predictions made by 284 people who made their living "commenting or offering advice on political and economic trends," and found they were actually worse than chance at predicting the future; their predictions would have been better if they had simply guessed at the outcome. But, Tetlock found, media pundits are often rewarded for their confidence and speaking ability, and develop ways of explaining away their mistakes, so they keep their jobs and stay on-screen.[11]

Tetlock established a dichotomy for forecasters based on a poem from the Greek poet Archilochus and made famous by the philosopher–political theorist Isaiah Berlin in 1953. On one hand, you have thinkers who act like foxes, according to Berlin, who know many things. On the other, you have hedgehogs who only know one big thing. Hedgehogs use their narrow scope of knowledge to form singular grand theories of the world, which they then use to create forecasts for events and phenomena (generally with below-average performance, Tetlock says). But foxes score high on his metrics. They synthesize information from many different fields and are skeptical of unifying theories that fall short of explaining edge cases: "thinkers who know many small things (tricks of their trade), are skeptical of grand schemes, ... and are rather diffident about their own forecasting prowess." By combining the predictive power of many different indicators—what the polls, economics, and demographics predict—models help us think more like foxes than hedgehogs. This is what makes good forecasters, by all accounts, better than the experts—whom Tetlock likens to dart-throwing monkeys.

The broader record of polling aggregation and election forecasting can be summed up by a popular quote attributed to the statistician George Box, who developed many of the methods that modelers use today: "All models are wrong, but some are useful." No mathematical formula or set of Monte Carlo simulations can capture the many complexities and interacting factors of our reality. The best we can hope is that a model approximates the truth closely enough to yield useful, actionable insights.

PAST PERFORMANCE DOES NOT GUARANTEE FUTURE RESULTS

To be useful, a model of polling data must at the very least capture the uncertainties inherent in conducting a survey. But since any given poll can be off the mark for a host of reasons—because of random chance, because it weighted one demographic too strongly, because it was conducted too early, because the question wording was slightly off, et cetera— it is impossible to know what the right amount of uncertainty is.

The overarching lesson from predictions of the 2016 and 2020 elections is that we are not always good at calculating the right value to represent this uncertainty. The polling model Natalie Jackson built stuck too close to the data, trusting pollsters to do the right thing and to match past performance. But a polling model that adds an arbitrary degree of uncertainty would also be "wrong" in George Box's eyes.

The standard practice is to analyze the historical record of the polls and set the uncertainty of the future equal to the uncertainty of the past. History, however, is not always a suitable guide to the realistic range of potential bias in the polls. When Donald Trump beat the FiveThirtyEight and *Huffington Post* forecasts in 2016, he did so in almost every state. His average overperformance was greater than any other candidate's since 2000, when pollsters began routinely polling state-level outcomes. The polls underestimated him more in redder states with more white voters who had not graduated from college, because many polls did not have enough of them in their samples; and worse, the ones they did get appeared to be more friendly to Democrats than was the case among actual voters.

In 2020, the average bias in the polls was even worse—indicating that the pattern of nonresponse had increased among right-leaning Americans. When I helped develop *The Economist*'s election-forecasting model in 2020, we included an adjustment for whether polls had the right share of Republicans and Democrats in them—polls we called "correctly balanced" by party identification or previous election results. This adjustment made our model better when tested on the 2016 election, but it did not work as well in reality as we had hoped. Our forecasts were only slightly less biased than Nate Silver's in red states, and we missed a surprising number of Trump's voters in Florida and the Midwest, since the polls there were most biased. As we will learn in the coming chapters, the Republicans who answered the polls were more likely to say they were going to vote for Joe Biden than the actual population of Republicans across America.

Polling aggregation is simply not capable of capturing changing dynamics of bias and adjusting for them. If all the data you are collecting are biased in the same direction, the forecast will have no choice but to be biased too. Models of polls cannot be that much wiser than the data they take in. As this problem gets worse, aggregators may be significantly underestimating the risk of electoral upsets by relying on past patterns of collective polling bias, which were less swayed by partisan nonresponse bias. Even worse, if only a few pollsters are following the "right" rules for public opinion research, they will be drowned out by the significant volume of less accurate polls, making the output of the aggregate worse than its inputs.

WHEN NATE SILVER STARTED FIVETHIRTYEIGHT.COM in 2008, the conventional wisdom surrounding polling aggregation was that it was nearly a sure bet on the outcome. We know now that that was wrong. Silver's championing of his model as being right in 50 out of 50 states in

2012 probably did not help. His reputation as an elections oracle may have led people to expect too much from the polls. Likewise, collective belief in the aggregation process has drifted too far, and falsely, toward seeing averages as a promise.

Where we go wrong in aggregation is in trusting that more data is always better. Silver's models, taking in his "secret sauce" formulation of pollster ratings and debiasing, might be appropriate for a subject such as baseball, where data are unbiased and the signal can be found within the noise (to borrow from the title of his 2012 book). But because the science on which polls are built is constantly evolving, reconsidering assumptions and correcting past errors, election forecasting will never approach the accuracy of, say, "moneyball"—with its precise measurements of a baseball player's skills and rich datasets of factors that impact performance.

The specific proposals that I have put to work in *The Economist*'s forecasting models include allowing more room for assessing bias from partisan nonresponse, lower-quality weighting schemes, and data collection, and relying more on non-polling factors to correct our judgments when samples are skewed. Elections are well predicted by variables political scientists refer to as the "fundamentals"—factors such as economic growth and presidential approval ratings. We can lean on these data when polls go astray. The best election models will also be open and transparent, and require very little human intervention and ad hoc adjustment.

The forecasts of the future will not improve on their record by endlessly massaging the polls to find their signal, but in allowing more room for us to fully accept their inherent noisiness. Consumers of polling and election models should not trick themselves into mistaking polls and projections for a science they're not—and will likely never be.

6

BIG DATA AND BLACK BOXES

The key to progress, innovation, and development of something better is approaching familiar problems with methods we have not used before or tackling problems we could not solve before. If something significant seems impossible then it is worthy of attention.

—WARREN MITOFSKY, "SCRUTINIZING OUR ACCEPTED PRACTICES," 1998

The internet reshaped political journalism. Giving pollsters and statisticians nearly instantaneous access to tens of millions of consumers ushered in an era of data-centered reporting on candidates and campaigns that would not have been possible otherwise.

The internet has also changed the way polls are conducted. The pulse of democracy is increasingly taken online, rather than by phone or in a face-to-face survey. In 2000, no major public poll was conducted online. By 2020, well over half of the surveys collected by Nate Silver's staff at

FiveThirtyEight, by then a major media outlet, were conducted over the internet.

The motivation for switching methods is clear. The last twenty years have brought major challenges for traditional telephone pollsters. The wider use of caller ID and the proliferation of spam calls mean that people are less inclined to answer calls from polling organizations. As a result, pollsters have experienced a precipitous decline in response rates. According to the Pew Research Center, only 7% of the calls they make are answered; In the 1970s, those numbers were as high as 70%. Estimates from other organizations calculate response rates that are even lower.

Declining response rates make it harder for pollsters to reach the number of people needed to ensure representativeness. Imagine that you are reaching again into that proverbial bag of 100 blue and yellow marbles for a sample of colors, but instead of finding 100 balls jumbling around in the bag, you only find ten; someone has removed the other ninety and given you a smaller bag! The law of large numbers implies you will now have a harder time picking an unbiased set of marbles, since the bag you hold could already have too many yellows or blues in it. If you take five marbles out, count the blues and yellows, place them back in the bag and repeat, the chance of selecting a diverse set of colors is much smaller than it would be if you had 100 to choose from. And you are also at risk of selecting the same marble multiple times.

The problem for pollsters is similar. As people become less likely to answer the phone, the chance that the people who are answering are statistically *weirder* than the population as a whole rises.

The widespread switch from home landline telephones to cellular devices is a compounding issue. Because federal regulations make it illegal to auto-dial cell phones, pollsters who want to call mobile users (a standard practice) have to pay workers to dial numbers manually, which is much more expensive. For pollsters who do the most diligence, the cost of a high-quality poll can run into the six figures. Only the most well-funded firms can achieve today what George Gallup and his colleagues did a century ago.

As a result, much of the innovation in polling over the last twenty years has come from political campaigns, with their deeper pockets and motivation to find more respondents. Pollsters are even using "big data" and machine learning tools in their twenty-first-century methods. The story here begins in a dark, damp boiler room deep inside Barack Obama's 2012 campaign headquarters in Chicago—a room they called the "data cave." Inside, an army of nerds applied modern statistical tools to classic problems of political science and public opinion polling. They changed the industry for the better.

BARACK OBAMA'S SECRET WEAPON

Erin Hartman is the unrecognized whiz kid of Barack Obama's 2012 reelection campaign. She revolutionized the way campaigns conduct their pre-election polls.

Hartman worked alongside an army of fifty other nerds for Obama's analytics team, a new subset of political campaign workers who are responsible for tracking the candidate's position in the polls, testing messages that could persuade and mobilize voters, forecasting the likely outcome of the election, and allocating resources to maximize the odds that the candidate will win. Hartman worked under Dan Wagner, the chief analytics officer, and contributed to the operation dubbed the "Victory Lab" by journalist Sasha Issenberg in his eponymously titled book about Obama's 2008 campaign.

Back then, Wagner and his team created the first individualized political campaign. As the National Get Out the Vote Targeting director, Wagner's job was to compile data on every registered voter in the country and produce two probabilistic scores for each of them: whether they would vote, and if so, whether they would support Obama or John McCain.

The campaign produced these scores with a three-step process. First, they obtained a list of every registered voter in the country from a database called the "voter file," which compiles information on each voter who has registered with each state's secretary of state. (Researchers can get these individual lists from most states for free, but there are several companies that will gather the files from all the states and combine them—for a fee, of course.) The voter file contains a list of each person's address, how old they are, their sex, their marital status, and (in some states) their race, among other characteristics. The voter file can also be merged with data on consumer behavior, such as whether someone has ever owned a car, what their television viewing habits are, or what their credit rating is. Wagner also used extra information on voters' preferences and habits that was compiled by previous campaigns, which often stored their data in a national database managed by the Democratic National Committee. The database also lists phone numbers, which made it convenient for the campaign to use for conducting a telephone poll in which they could know exactly who they were talking to. Pollsters call this "registration-based sampling," often abbreviated as RBS.[1]

The second step of the campaign's scoring process was to call as many people as possible and ask them who they were voting for. During some weeks, the campaign contacted over 5,000 voters in each battleground state, giving it a massive set of data on Obama's supporters. Wagner merged this polling data with his information from the voter file so he could know what a person's demographic profile was, where they were from, if they voted in the past, and whether they would vote for Obama in 2008. All of this information gave the campaign enough data to make a pretty good guess as to whether someone was a voter and, if so, whether they tended to vote for Democrats.

But "pretty good" is not good enough for the science of elections. For their third and final step, the campaign programmed computer models ("algorithms") that predicted each person's likelihood of supporting the would-be president, based on the data it had collected on interviewees so far—up to 1,000 variables in some cases. These models could be used to make predictions about people the campaign had not contacted yet. If the campaign identified a "persuadable" voter, they could send a team of canvassers out to their house to ask them if they were going to vote and to see if they could get them to commit to Obama. If the canvassers were successful, they would log information about the conversation on a mobile phone program that fed data back to the campaign's computer models. If the algorithm was wrong and identified a nonvoter or a John McCain supporter as persuadable, that information could also be used to recalibrate the prediction model.

GRANULAR ELECTORAL DATA has a long history in election campaigns. As far back as the middle of the twentieth century, strategists had figured out that focusing their efforts on marginal precincts with a lot of voters was key to their success. But this was the first time a campaign focused so much attention on the individual voters themselves. The 2008 Obama campaign perfected something that politics nerds call "microtargeting," a way to predict how individual voters feel about candidates. Insiders were used to thinking of campaigns as organisms, constantly evolving in needs, capabilities, and structure. Dan Wagner went beyond, teaching analysts how to look deeper, to the atomic level. By 2012, the Obama team's data gurus were the Simulmatics Corporation on steroids.

Inside "the cave," computer fans buzzed and human minds whirled to come up with new ways of solving the various statistical problems required to predict the voting behavior of over 150 million registered voters. The team used machine learning techniques and analyzed "big data" to target every likely convert in the country and contact the disengaged adults who had never participated in politics before. Fueling it all was a constant stream of new polling data about the electorate.

Erin Hartman was in charge of collecting that data. As the head of analytics polling for the most advanced election campaign in history, she set the standard for polling in the twenty-first century. While finishing her PhD in political science at the University of California, Berkeley, Hartman was brought on board to help build a computer program (which the campaign later called "the optimizer") that identified what television programs the most persuadable voters were watching, so they could target them with advertisements. If the ideal "persuadables" were 45-year-old white women without a college degree, the campaign would book ads on local television stations during the programs they watched most frequently.

Hartman moved to campaign headquarters in Chicago in July 2011. When her supervisor left the campaign because of a family emergency toward the end of 2011, Dan Wagner incorporated the optimizer into his broader analytics team umbrella and made Hartman the director of all campaign polling.

Hartman quickly spotted inefficiencies in how the campaign was conducting its polling. Response rates were much lower than expected, which made data more expensive and models more prone to error. By comparing the polls to administrative data and actual election results, the campaign could tell that nonrespondents were different from people who picked up the phone; they were less educated, less politically engaged, younger, and had different attitudes on a range of issues. But without being able to ask the nonrespondents what they thought about politics, it was impossible to quantify the mismatch.

Hartman had the industry-changing idea to use the information from the voter file to predict whether someone would pick up the phone. "Well, from building all these targeting models we can predict pretty well who you're gonna vote for with pretty high accuracy," Hartman recalls saying to Wagner at the time. "I can take some of those ideas to predict whether or not you're going to respond to a survey.... I can use that information to improve our sampling designs."[2]

Because the campaign's pollsters had been calling off the voter file, they knew whether or not an individual who was called in a previous poll had picked up the phone. That is the chief advantage of an RBS poll over a traditional phone poll that uses random-digit dialing (RDD) technology. "In RDD," Hartman says, "you know who you get, you know who responds, but you don't know who doesn't respond. [Polling off] the voter file allows you to characterize who doesn't respond to surveys and think about ways to account for that information."[3]

With the hundreds of thousands of people the Obama campaign had called so far, they could use their demographic and political attributes to calculate nonresponse scores for everyone else in the voter file. Just as the team for the 2008 campaign had continuously trained their models to investigate the relationships between demographics and support for Obama, Hartman could train a model to predict whether someone would pick up the phone.

LEAVING THE CAVE

Armed with the campaign's big data and a type of machine learning algorithm called a "classification tree," which automatically learns the relationships between certain variables of interest, Hartman's team could figure out if some types of people would be harder to poll than others. Then, when they were randomly selecting people off the voter file to start calling them—what pollsters call "drawing a sample"—they would just pick more of the people who would be less likely to respond, so that the nonrespondents would, in aggregate, be more likely to be represented by the final polling.

The precise math here is relatively easy: you just sample at a rate "inversely proportional" to the probability of responding; mathematically, the number of people to call who match a certain profile is equal to 1 divided by the probability of a person of that profile responding. For example, if the Erin Hartmans of the world—young white women who owned a cell phone and lived in a metro area—responded to a poll only about 10% of the time, the pollsters would just place ten times as many calls to them: $1 \div 0.10 = 10$. For every Erin Hartman you want in your data set, you need to call ten. Repeating this process for every person in the voter file would improve the campaign's shot at getting hard-to-reach people to tell them who they were going to vote for.

This innovation is called "response rate sampling." It had two primary benefits for Hartman. First, it decreased the amount of weighting that she had to do to bring the percentage of each demographic group in its poll in line with its share of the voting population, as measured by their "true" distribution in the voter file. Because the team was calling more respondents who had a lower propensity to answer the phone, they had a higher chance of gathering data from hard-to-reach voters, like young people. By decreasing the weight that her computer program assigned to that group when calculating results, the campaign could be surer of the poll's accuracy, since the uncertainty of a poll increases with the amount of weighting you do to it.

Second, and perhaps more importantly, Hartman's innovation ensured that the attitudes of nonrespondents on the issues and the candidates were represented in the poll. If nonrespondents were two percentage points more likely to support Romney than responders, a normal poll would imply that Obama's position was safer than it seemed. Hartman's version would probably be more accurate. In the end, the campaign's efforts were highly successful. One of the team's models predicted that Obama would win 57.7% of the early vote in Hamilton County, Ohio. In reality, he won 57.2%—an error of just half a percentage point.[4]

In a perfect world, Erin Hartman's work for Barack Obama's reelection campaign would have been tried out immediately by every telephone pollster in the country. Her response-rate sampling had massive potential to reduce bias caused by "differential partisan nonresponse," in which members of one political party are much less likely to take a poll than members of the other. If patterns were predictable based on the variables pollsters had at their disposal, such as age, race, education, income, party, and geography, nonresponse could nearly become a nonissue. Although political pollsters would still have to conduct traditional RDD telephone polls to sample the attitudes of Americans who are not registered to vote and therefore do not show up in states' voter files, any pre-election polling would ideally still be mixed with polls conducted off the voter file in order to adjust nonresponse biases among the voting population.

But the world of public opinion research is far from ideal. First, not every polling outfit has access to a voter file. Subscriptions can be very expensive, often more expensive than the added cost of calling people who won't respond to your poll. Reengineering statistical models to incorporate the new methods also takes time, which many firms do not have. Further, many pollsters clinging to RDD phone polls would not have the technical know-how to make the switch even if they tried; Hartman and her colleagues were in a league of their own when it came to their programming and statistical abilities.

An added difficulty is that nonresponse, as it turns out, is not so easily predictable. Nate Cohn, the *New York Times*'s pollster, adopted a version of Hartman's method in 2020 and still overestimated Joe Biden's vote margin by five percentage points in Pennsylvania, six in Florida, four in North Carolina, and five in Michigan, only barely exceeding the accuracy of the average poll in those states.[5] One theory is that state-mandated lockdowns to stop the spread of the covid-19 virus made Democrats more likely to stay home, and they disproportionately live in areas with high population density and are more likely than Republicans to have college educations and white-collar jobs they can do remotely. This, in turn, may have made them more likely to pick up the phone. This new pandemic-fueled pattern of heightened partisan nonresponse would have been hard to pick up in historical data. Further, it is hard to capture the full cause of the nonresponse with data. Cohn, for example, used a person's registered party affiliation as the primary partisan variable in his models. But if only the subset of registered Republicans who supported President Donald Trump were likely to refuse pollsters' calls, the model wouldn't have detected the bias.[6]

Despite the mixed success of response-rate adjusted polling, the method is nevertheless the most sophisticated approach yet to deal with the problem of low response rates to telephone polls. But in the twenty-first century, pollsters are not stuck with calling people on their land-lines or smartphones any longer. The internet offers a multitude of new approaches to measuring the average American.

DIALING VERSUS DIAL-UP

Polling firms that conduct their surveys online can collect interviews from thousands of Americans very quickly, and usually at a fraction of the cost of telephone polls. They do not have to hire people to punch in tens of thousands of cell phone numbers at a call center. There are many ways to recruit participants; you can pay people to visit your website and give them polls to fill out, advertise a survey on social media platforms, and send emails or text messages directing people to an online link. Many people will even give you their data for free, or treat survey-taking as a sort of game to pass the time, usually in exchange for a chance to win a prize. Some online polling firms incentivize survey-taking with a point system; once you fill out enough surveys, you can redeem points for a dis-counted movie ticket or a coupon to Waffle House.

Online polls also provide a few advantages over traditional polls in terms of what you can learn about participants. Instead of randomly calling members of the public to take one-off surveys, never to be inter-viewed again, platforms for online polls can easily be used to conduct repeat questioning of the same individuals in order to understand their behavior over time. Instead of creating a polling aggregation model of many different data points, in which individual polls could vary in their estimates for any number of reasons, so-called panel surveys let research-ers detect real shifts in the public by interviewing people multiple times. If someone tells you they used to vote for Democrats but now they prefer Republicans, you know that they're actually changing their mind (or at least that they're claiming to). A polling aggregate, in contrast, can be swayed by a bunch of Republicans refusing to answer the polls, a change in methodology, or any number of statistical design flukes. Online polls also provide more room for experimentation—the big online firms run parallel businesses that conduct normal political polls but also let academics conduct studies about how certain psychological cues, response options, or the wording of a question can change the way people respond to polls. Being asked about "the state of the nation's economy" may elicit a different answer than, say, "the economic health of the country." Survey experiments give researchers scientific tools with which they can figure out answers to these questions and improve the art of polling.

The big danger of online polls, however, is that they are not statistically representative of the broader population. Not everyone has internet access—and the people who do are more likely to be rich and white than the people who do not. Although some online pollsters use advanced statistical methods to try to get samples that are as representative as possible, many data-collection vendors are largely experimental, and the data they collect are clearly not representative of the public. Despite the appealing idea that "big data" and statistical methods can be leveraged to learn about the population from a small sample of online data, the evidence shows that, as one pollster told me long ago, "you can't weight your way out of bad data." An online survey has to be carefully designed if it's going to compete with the accuracy of a (twentieth-century, high-quality, high response rate) RDD phone poll, or one of Hartman's or Cohn's voter file–based surveys today.

DOUG RIVERS IS THE CHIEF SCIENTIST for YouGov, the best known and among the most accurate online pollsters. If George Gallup is the founder of "scientific" polling, Rivers holds a similar title for high-quality online polls.

Rivers was first exposed to political polling in his final undergraduate year at Columbia. One of his professors arranged for him to work temporarily for the elections division at CBS News. It was then run by Warren Mitofsky, the statistician who invented random-digit dialing and pioneered the nationwide exit poll. There were few better fits for an enter-prising, young, soon-to-be pollster. But it took Rivers a few decades to fully realize his potential, and he didn't do any formal work on polling until the '90s.

Rivers graduated from Columbia in 1977 as a budding econometri-cian with a passing interest in statistics. After deciding he didn't want to be a lawyer, he went into academia. In 1981, he graduated with his PhD from Harvard and joined its faculty as an assistant professor. The econo-metrics field at that time was exploding with new methods of empiri-cal research. He got to study measurement error and selection bias—two things that "really agreed with" him—and had unearthed many appli-cations to political science. "I was a kid in a candy store" for shopping around for more methods, he told me.[7]

Rivers went on to teach at the California Institute of Technology, the research university in Pasadena, as well as University of California, Los Angeles, and Stanford, where he has been a professor since 1989. At UCLA, he was part of the college's first statistics program, organized by the dean of social science and renowned political psychologist Dave Sears.

In 1986, Rivers had his second run-in with polling and election work. He submitted a research paper to a team of survey scientists supervising the American National Election Study (ANES), a large national survey run by the University of Michigan's Institute for Social Research and Survey Research Center (the organization that popularized "area prob-ability" sampling in the 1940s and 1950s). Rivers had developed a new method to make the ANES's Senate elections samples more representa-tive. Before 1986, the poll was designed to represent the demographics of the United States, but failed at hitting key state-level benchmarks. Bias was especially bad in smaller states. Rivers's redesign was so successful that the ANES asked him to be on their board of directors in 1987.

In 1988, Rivers was hired by Arthur Andersen Economics, a con-sulting arm of the national accounting firm. He was to help design an audit of a chain of psychiatric hospitals that had been corruptly managed and owed the United States government thousands of dollars. He told the accounting firm how to select the sample of clinics to estimate the approximate amount of money they had to pay. However, according to Rivers, the Federal Bureau of Investigation halted the study two days into data collection to conduct their own inquiry.

Years later, while teaching at Stanford, Rivers began attending statistics seminars, which he found more interesting than econometrics. He grew increasingly interested in how to fix the sampling methods of public polling firms and market research organizations that had started conducting surveys online, and in his opinion were quite bad at it. For example, Harris Interactive had been sending surveys to a random selection of users of the search engine excite.com (later eclipsed by Google). But according to Rivers, Harris had allegedly been sending surveys to millions of excite.com users, which would have constituted an unrepresentative sample. That's because the population of internet users in the late 1990s tended to skew young, rich, and white. But since not every internet user knew about excite, Harris was faced with similar issues as the *Literary Digest* in 1936: a large sample size did not fix underlying problems of representation.

Other companies were also experimenting with ways to recruit people to take surveys over the internet by mailing invitations to a random subset of households. The problem with their approach, according to Rivers, was that too few internet users would respond, and the surveyors often ended up assigning demographic quotas to try and make them representative. Market researchers typically used quota sampling to adjust the demographic breakdowns of their surveys, but that practice is a big no-no to people like Rivers, who had been trained in statistics and scientific sampling methods.

In the late 1990s, the Nielsen Company, famous for its measurement of viewership for various TV channels and programs, bought a startup called NetRatings to randomly sample people over the internet. They used random-digit dialing to reach thousands of households over the

phone, and installed tracking software on willing participants' computers to log the websites they visited.[8] This, too, is problematic: the type
of people who are willing to be tracked, and already own the computer
hardware, might not be representative of the population.

Rivers and his colleague Norman Nie spotted a hole in the market.
If they could create a more statistically sound panel—a group of people
willing to take repeated surveys over the internet—the improved accuracy and marketing material might help them beat the competition. In
1998, they received funding from a group of venture capital firms to get
their new company, Intersurvey, off the ground.

The idea at first seemed foolproof. "Why don't we recruit a real probability sample via random-digit dialing," Rivers recalls thinking, "pay
them a modest amount for their time, and give them WebTV devices to
fill out surveys at home?" WebTV was a company that manufactured a
device that plugged into a person's television set to provide them with
internet access, a setup that is similar to the way desktop computers plug
into their own dedicated monitors. "Then we'll have a random sample of
people on the internet instead of a random sample of excite.com users."
Instead of answering the phone when it rang, respondents would get a
signal on their WebTV device that meant it was time for them to fill
out a poll.[9]

Intersurvey's technology had a few key advantages over the competition. First, because it provided internet access to a random sample
of Americans, it met the standards of probability statistics. Intersurvey
could also get quick feedback on any number of questions; whereas a
typical poll took days to conduct, a poll using WebTV boxes could be
done in a few hours (or even a few minutes, if a smaller sample was
acceptable). And the WebTV devices were also relatively inexpensive,
costing just $149 a pop. Intersurvey had amassed 100,000 panelists by
2000. That year, the company changed its name to Knowledge Networks to be more appetizing to market researchers. The firm is still
around today.

The idea was sound. The execution of the business concept, however, had some serious drawbacks. The big challenge was attrition: people fell off the panel over time. Although plenty of people were willing to take the TV polls for $10—which was how much Intersurvey paid them when they were first contacted—they would quickly go silent. Rivers estimates that Knowledge Networks could get about 50% of young people to join the panel, but of the people who were sent devices, only 50% would actually connect them, and 50% of that group would quit immediately after the first survey. Then, you'd lose a certain percentage every month. The result, calculated by Knowledge Networks in 2001, was that only 2% of the initial sample were still answering questions after one year.

Rivers figured he could get the response rate up to 5% by offering people more money, but that rate was still too low to be cost-effective. Besides, increasing overhead expenses to keep panelists from leaving would not have fixed any biases resulting from the initial selection process. Even with a sample that was drawn using random probability sampling, it was very likely that the people who weren't answering the phone or who subsequently refused the initial recruitment offers were systematically different from those who joined, and in ways they couldn't fully account for. The heightened potential for bias was untenable for a statistician. "That's a joke," Rivers said. "A 2% or a 5% response rate is not a probability sample. Anyone who tells you that is lying to themselves. It still may be the right way to do it," he said, but the claims of accuracy "are total BS."[10] If you didn't know the real uncertainty in the sample, how could you be sure you actually knew anything about the population?

This was the real nail in the coffin for the methodology of the Knowledge Networks panel. Between the high-quality RDD sample and WebTV equipment, Rivers told me that the company was spending up to $30 per interview—around $25,000 for a typical poll—when some of its competitors could provide a sample of essentially equal quality at $7 per person. "So the sample isn't representative. It doesn't match the expectations from market research firms. And it's expensive for what it is," Rivers recalls thinking to himself. A Silicon Valley entrepreneur at heart, he concluded it was time to move on to "the next big thing."

WEB 2.0

Doug Rivers was driving to Stanford University's campus in Palo Alto, California, in the fall of 2003 when it occurred to him: you could mix a telephone and online poll together to increase sample size and reduce bias. The probability sample would provide the demographic benchmarks on which a massive amount of online data would be re-weighted, leveraging the power of each mode to reach different populations.

According to Rivers, Knowledge Networks was not interested in adopting his new methods, so he struck off on his own. He got investment capital from one of Knowledge Networks' investors and then called up half a dozen of his friends at mainstream polling firms and asked them for a favor. He would pay them $1 for each interview they were conducting if, at the end of all their calls, they would ask respondents to provide their email addresses. Then, Rivers could email them a link to his own survey. This group of recruits would form the backbone of his new online polling business, which he called Polimetrix. He would also recruit survey-takers online—for example, via Google Ads—spending far less than it would cost to conduct phone interviews. Rivers would "do the magic" on the combined sample and sell the findings to interested companies.

The experiment was a huge success. Rivers found that by crafting ads carefully, Polimetrix could harvest millions of respondents to short surveys very cheaply. The click-through rates on their survey advertisements were so high (around 15%) that Google later hired the UCLA student who had worked on them. The most successful ads were faux polls that ran alongside scandalous content, such as accounts of Martha Stewart's insider trading trial or the allegations of child molestation against Michael Jackson. Polimetrix ran an ad that asked "WHO'S GUILTY?" which, if clicked, would send a user to their website, ask them to fill out a quick survey, and then enroll them in their panel. Because nobody else was buying ad space on negative scandals, Google AdWords (the company's system for displaying ads on webpages) was basically free.

Polimetrix's poll was a data geek's dream. It was cheap, massive, and had few problems aside from the troubling fact that it recruited a sample that was too engaged in the news and politics (Rivers alleges it wasn't any worse than the samples pollsters got over the phone). As long as you didn't use it to study things that were correlated with political participation, like donating to or volunteering for campaigns, it was fine. Rivers had a hard time selling space on the panel to political pollsters, who were reluctant to move online, but it was a massively profitable enterprise for market research.

By 2006, Doug Rivers had discovered a few methodological issues with Polimetrix's data-collection procedures. First, in an all-too-familiar story, response rates to telephone polls had sunk too low to ensure that the people recruited into the online panel were representative of the population. For example, the panel (via the adjustments to make it match phone polls) had a higher percentage of students than it should have had, tilting the sample to the left and biasing other statistics such as the unemployment rate.

The weighting algorithm that pollsters usually used—a technique called "raking"—was also messing up his data. With raking it is possible to make sure a poll is representative by gender, for example, by specifying the right percentage of females and letting the algorithm do its thing. You can also ensure a right balance by age, race, or anything else you have. But if you don't have the target breakdowns for the interactions *between* these variables—the share of the population who should be female *and* over 65 years old, for example—you can still end up with pretty wrong estimates. And if you "rake" to both of these variables, you risk overfitting the algorithm—if you end up with just one female senior, for example, that individual can be given too much weight in the sample (because the population of seniors in reality is not 100% female).

Rivers's solution was to use a new technique called "sample match-ing," which allowed him to take many variables into account. Instead of sampling randomly from a list of telephone numbers, or filling quo-tas for different groups, sample matching is a three-step procedure that lets researchers get a small, representative sample out of a larger, non-representative pool of respondents. For example, for a poll of all Ameri-can adults, Rivers might first use the decennial United States census to determine how many people in each category of race, age, gender, and education there are in the population. Perhaps 10% of adults are white males younger than 40 who have a college education, and 12% are women of the same demographic.

Rivers would next randomly pick 1,000 of these different types of people in a way that ensures their demographics roughly match the characteristics of the full population. He calls this the "target sample." Then, for each archetyp-ical respondent in the target sample, he selects one member of the online opt-in poll who matches it (either exactly or with respect to the vast majority of traits). Then he sends that group, the "matched sample," an email to ask them to take a survey. This process ensures that the poll sample is demographically representative of the target population, so long as there is no uncorrected bias in (a) who responds or (b) the sample of people taking polls on the internet. One advantage of this method is that if one person doesn't respond, you can select a different individual with the same traits to fill their place. This con-trasts with both RDD and RBS polls. In a traditional random-digit-dialed telephone poll, you don't know who is on the other end of the line and you don't get a second chance to call them back. And though you can call nonre-spondents back if your poll uses registration-based sampling, there's nothing you can do if they continue to ignore your calls.

Throughout 2006 and 2007, Rivers worked on a deal to sell Polimetrix to a UK market research company called YouGov, which was looking to expand its online polling operations to other countries. Rivers took an offer to run the company's US operations in exchange for stock options; later, he took on a different role, as the company's chief scientist.

At YouGov, Rivers has continued to push the boundaries of what's possible with online polls, sharpening tools to take the public's pulse in the twenty-first century. He has adopted some of Erin Hartman's work modeling nonresponse with classification trees, and is an enthusiastic early adopter of an alternative weighting method called "multilevel regression with post-stratification" (MRP), which we will return to in the next section. He has also incorporated voter files as his basis for re-weighting surveys, bringing online polls closer to representing the world of registered voters. Rivers claims that YouGov has a much better picture of what the electorate looks like than any other pollster. He may be right; as of 2020, YouGov's polling is just as accurate at predicting elections—if not more so—than the most sophisticated live-interviewer phone polls that use "probability" sampling methods.

And other firms are coming around to the idea that online polls are good enough for their research. The Pew Research Center, which had experienced ballooning costs of telephone research (often exceeding $100,000 per poll), has switched to collecting nearly the entirety of their data via its own method of online polling with probability samples. They use address-based sampling, in which a pollster mails envelopes with $10 or $20 to a random sample of American households and asks respondents to fill out the polls online. The University of Chicago's National Opinion Research Center—established in 1941—also set up their own probability online panel in 2014. They called it "AmeriSpeak." Major media outlets, such as the *Washington Post*, now regularly work with online pollsters, such as Ipsos. Public opinion polling, at long last, has entered the twenty-first century.

STIRRING THE POT

In the Obama campaign's data cave on Election Day 2012, things were not looking so good. "It was 10:30am . . . and my numbers were telling me that President Obama might lose Ohio," Yair Ghitza, a data scientist for a voter-file vendor called Catalist, recounts in his PhD dissertation. Data on turnout had come in, and his modeling showed that young people and minorities were turning out at lower rates than they had expected:

> I remember one senior analyst's ominous interpretation: "it looked like this could be real." Another analyst, extremely sharp but perhaps prone to dramatic swings, memorably declares "We're fucked." A senior member of the team excused himself, and I later found out that he proceeded immediately to the bathroom, in order to vomit.[11]

Ghitza's thesis reports on a group of projects related to statistical modeling and political science. He had been hired by the Obama campaign roughly six weeks before the election to program a model that could predict how the election was unfolding throughout the day, based on the way turnout among different groups was looking. Ghitza was interested in answering two questions: First, "Could we measure deviations from expected turnout for different groups of the electorate in real time?" And second: "Could we redirect our mobilization efforts to compensate and maximize our chance of winning the election?"

Obtaining answers to these two questions is, as it turns out, extremely hard. Ghitza told me that it took nearly all of the six weeks he worked for the campaign to come up with a solution that they were reasonably sure would not break down on Election Day. Because nobody had ever done this before, they were trying to solve the problem from scratch. They also lacked any real-time data on who was voting, and so had to calibrate the model to anecdotal reports from the campaign. Imagine attempting to calculate the area of a circle without ever being taught geometry, and without anyone who can tell you if you're on the right track.

The result of his toiling was a system of prediction that was probably right, but came with plenty of uncertainty. Ghitza took the data seriously when it told him on the morning of November 6, 2012, that the campaign was going to lose Ohio—but he wasn't swayed so far as to think Obama would lose the whole election. David Shor, Ghitza's colleague who created the campaign's pre-election poll-based forecasts, later remarked, "That was the worst 12 hours of my life."[12]

Ghitza was not hired by the Obama campaign to work on its voter file and polling operation, but he probably should have been. He had studied breakthrough statistical modeling during his doctoral work at Columbia, developing a lot of the methods his current employer, Catalist, uses to merge polls with voter files and model support for political candidates at the individual level. The hallmark method of his dissertation, "multilevel regression with post-stratification" (MRP), was thought up by his advisor, Andrew Gelman, in the 1990s. It is now the statistical back end for the next generation of online polls, including the ones conducted by Doug Rivers.

Sometimes called "Mister P," the method is an alternative way of weighting a poll. It is especially useful when a researcher wants to turn a national sample into estimates of sub-national opinion, for example, turning an election poll into predictions for all fifty states and the District of Columbia. MRP accomplishes this by first running a statistical model on the raw polling data to quantify the precise impacts of a person's age, education, race, income, home state, and what have you on the variable a pollster is interested in—such as who they're going to vote for or whether they approve of the president's job performance. Then, using data from the Census Bureau on how many people of each demographic type live in each state, a researcher can predict the approximate number of, say, Obama voters in each state, and can forecast the outcome of the election. The technique could also be used to estimate state-level opinion on issue positions or public policy, an area where political data journalists are beginning to make progress.

YouGov has used MRP to create a thorough portrait of the demographics and political traits of American voters. By combining the standard Census Bureau data with another of its high-response-rate surveys on political participation and the voter file, their polls can control for many more traits than a traditional phone poll, which lacks both the best statistical methods and the information necessary to know how many Americans of each party there are in each demographic group.

But what if you could run Mister P for every voter in the United States, individually? That is the focus of Ghitza's most recent work. At Catalist, he leads a team that mixes surveys of hundreds of thousands of voters with individual records of voter turnout and demographic attributes to come up with estimates of political behavior—which candidate voters supported in the 2016 or 2020 elections, for example—for every single person. Ghitza's dissertation also focused on methods to measure the uncertainty of his MRP models. After the 2018 midterms, Catalist released their projection from a similar model as an alternative to the post-election exit polls that the news networks conducted. Thanks to MRP, the type of work that would have previously taken hundreds of surveys interviewing tens of thousands of voters in different states and congressional districts across the country can instead be conducted using one large, national survey and running models on the underlying data to make projections for the whole population.

DREW LINZER HAS BEEN USING a similar approach to Ghitza's and YouGov's at his polling firm, Civiqs, since 2013. He started the outfit after giving up his job as a professor of public opinion at Emory University and moving across the country to the San Francisco Bay Area. Civiqs is a part of Kos Media, which runs the Daily Kos website and other advocacy and research organizations for progressive causes.

Civiqs is focused on two issues that concern polling firms. Firms ask the same questions in different surveys for different clients, duplicating work across costly telephone samples. And because survey companies are driven by their clients' needs, public opinion is only recorded when and where a client wants to conduct research.

Linzer, who had a background in survey sampling and election fore-casting models, thought to himself, "Why don't we free ourselves from that constraint and do the research all the time?" The firm could send questions to a representative sample matched from a large online panel (similar to YouGov's) every day, "pulling down" results from the Civiqs servers whenever someone wanted to pay for the results. They could also add separate questions based on clients' desires and measure change over time—often detecting trends before other pollsters even had the idea to look for them.

While the idea behind Civiqs is simple, the implementation is one of the most complex experiments in polling in decades. The goal is to recruit a large national panel and automate the process of conducting opinion surveys, making sure that the design is "sustainable over a long period of time, interviewing every day, on as many different questions that peo-ple would be interested in." Linzer says his team is extra careful not to send too many questions to a panelist, which might cause them to leave. He emphasizes that this is all done behind the scenes by computers, free of human intervention. The design of that infrastructure costs millions of dollars. Civiqs also invests in recruiting panelists from hard-to-reach groups, which are underrepresented by less sophisticated online polls.[13]

Even after getting a large, robust, interested sample, Civiqs needs to adjust the data to control for nonresponse from certain groups by making the demographic and political breakdown of the sample match the num-bers in the population as a whole. The models Linzer created to adjust his samples are some of the most complex in the business. Described as a "dynamic MRP model," the programming feeding Civiqs' estimates is novel in that it allows the poll's numbers to change over time. While most pollsters run separate polls each time they're interested in a topic, Linzer's model collapses Civiqs' daily surveys into one giant "poll" and allows groups' attitudes to change over the course of the process. He is, in effect, creating a polling average straight out of the raw polling data. The underlying statistical model is so complex that it can take over a day to run for each question, depending on how long the firm has been asking the question. (Re-weighting data using the traditional raking algorithm, in contrast, would take mere seconds.)

Linzer's polling firm provides two primary benefits over other pollsters: speed and depth. Because they conduct new interviews on a question every day, they can publish updated results from new surveys in only two or three days' time. A traditional phone polling firm takes at least a week to design a questionnaire, field a survey, adjust the data, and write the reports. In contrast, Civiqs' estimates (for certain publicly released questions) are immediately posted to their website, where anyone can explore them. Gathering interviews is also cheaper online.

The Civiqs data also beats traditional polling models in providing estimates of opinion for small groups. Due to the use of MRP, the firm models attitudes for all combinations of demographic groups a client might be interested in, and for each day they have been asking the questions. Want to know how a 34-year-old white Democrat from Texas feels about gun control—and how their opinion has changed over time? Civiqs can tell you in an instant, while a normal poll would never have the proper sample size or trend. This amounts to a vastly more informative tool for storytelling. And according to Linzer, his firm isn't making "any sacrifices in accuracy" to accomplish these feats. In 2018 and 2020, their surveys were roughly as accurate as anyone else's.

EVERY POLL IS A MODEL

The model-driven approach to polling has left public opinion researchers with a lot of tough questions about data quality and uncertainty. The idea that you can create representative estimates with unrepresentative data relies on researchers fulfilling the chief assumption of MRP and other models: that if you have enough information about the population as a whole, you can reduce the bias of the sample. But what if, for example, students are overrepresented in polls, biasing the data toward a candidate popular with younger voters, but the pollster lacks information about how many students should be in the poll?

In contrast, the historical view of a "design-based" poll "(to adopt a dichotomy noted by the *Times*'s Nate Cohn), such as a pre-election survey that uses probability sampling to reach people over the phone, is that it wouldn't necessarily suffer from this problem.[14] The theory behind random sampling is that if you sample enough people, enough times, you will eventually approximate a representative sample of the population—so long as you have a few benchmarks for important population characteristics, such as the age and racial breakdown of the sample. And once you have enough random samples, you can just average them together. The aggregate survey, in theory, should be the best estimate. A design-based poll, in theory, would not need to consider as many sources of biases as an MRP-driven poll.

In practice, model-based and design-based polls suffer from similar weaknesses. Probability telephone polling, history has shown, is not as infallible as the theory suggests. In fact, one fluke of the weighting methods that old-school pollsters usually rely on is that they can give extremely high weights to underrepresented people in the sample. This makes them prone to wide variations from survey to survey. Just by random chance, for example, getting a respondent with wildly counterintuitive views can meaningfully change the result of a poll that has included too many interactions in its raking algorithm. Or a poll that has not decided to weight by an important variable—such as whether someone has a college education or not—might be biased over and over if non-college-educated voters aren't picking up the phone.

The proof here is in the pudding. In 2020, pre-election surveys from CNN and the survey firm SSRS oscillated wildly during the late spring and summer. In April, their surveys showed Joe Biden leading Donald Trump by 11 percentage points. The next month, he was only up by 5, and then by June he was leading by an even larger margin than in the spring: 14 points. Meanwhile, the average of polls had not changed very much.

Data from YouGov, Civiqs, and other model-based polls were much more stable.

To understand why this happened, it is helpful to look at a high-profile methodological mistake from the 2016 election. The *Los Angeles Times* and researchers at the University of Southern California released a daily tracking poll of the presidential race. Each morning, social scientists in USC's labs would pool together interviews that thousands of Americans submitted to them online. The poll was a worthy experiment in a new frontier of political polling—online panels of respondents—but it soon became apparent that there were two major anomalies. First, its daily gyrations were much more severe than one would expect. Was the country really so indecisive? Other polls didn't seem to gyrate as dramatically. Second, the tracking poll was wildly more pro-Trump than other polls. But the methodology was sound. The poll was run by top-notch researchers. How could this be?

The results seemed so odd that the poll became the subject of a hefty amount of journalistic inquiry. Upon examination, the *New York Times* found a culprit: the very statistical weighting that was meant to protect the poll against biased data was going haywire. In an effort to maintain a healthy racial composition of respondents, USC's algorithms were counting the opinions of one Black Midwestern man thirty times more than the typical respondent. Whoever he supported received a massive boost. For most of the campaign, this mystery man favored Donald Trump for the presidency. But in late October, he changed his mind—and overnight, the entire poll turned four percentage points more pro-Clinton. The swing tipped researchers off, but smaller, more frequent oscillations should have been a red flag all along.[15]

THE ERA OF PURELY DESIGN-BASED POLLING is now in the rearview mirror; all polls currently use some kind of modeling (raking, after all, is a form of modeling) to correct for potential bias in their data. So the question is really over what model one chooses. Statistical savants such as

Doug Rivers, Yair Ghitza, and Drew Linzer believe that MRP's sophistication is better suited to handle the particular challenges of polling, such as the interactions between demographic variables or nonresponse within particular demographic categories. An MRP model can also pick out the precise combination of variables that is leading someone to not answer the phone, for example, while the traditional raking algorithm that is used for weighting polls is ill-suited for this task.

But MRP cannot fix nonresponse if the pollster doesn't know where to look or what to adjust to. Although raking for too many factors in a design-based poll with a small number of respondents can cause it to swing around like crazy—what statisticians call high "variance"—a poll that is poorly designed and instead relies exclusively on modeling can suffer from a high level of bias—if, for example, Black voters were particularly unlikely to approve of a candidate, but you forgot to include the race variable in your model. That's one reason why the well-known MRP pollsters typically have larger samples than traditional phone pollsters: tabulating more interviews allows them to control for more variables that might cause bias.

Observers who decry model-driven polls for their failure to meet traditional standards of probability polling fail to realize that it is not the adjustment technique that is making polls more susceptible to errors but the fact that response rates are so low. And this problem affects design-based polls too. Twenty years ago, it was easier to conduct a telephone poll that reached a representative sample and needed less weighting to bring the share of low-education, low-income, and low-trust respondents (all are factors that decrease response rates today) in line with the population as a whole. But in a world in which many different adjustments must be made to a poll—of any source, via any method—it is easy for any one type of respondent to slip through the cracks. As a result, modeling is a necessity.

So, which is best, a well-designed poll or a well-modeled one? Pollsters have attempted to solve the trade-off between bias (which is higher when a model of biased polling data accounts for too few important variables) and variance (when a poll with too few respondents tries to account for too many) by comparing their predictions against reality. But in pre-election polling, there are not enough results from enough elections to decide what the "best" model is. And the answer is different from year to year as the nature of nonresponse changes. In 1948, pollsters had to worry about getting enough addresses for low-income voters. In 2016, they had too few Republicans. Pollsters might know which best practices to follow in general, but there is no way to know which practice itself is best.

The answer is that both ends of the model-driven, design-based spectrum suffer from error; it just shows up differently. A pollster has to choose the right mix of errors resulting from high variance and high bias regardless of method or mindset. Those statisticians we met in the introductory chapter, who found that the true margin of error for a poll was about twice the size as pollsters typically report, said the total seven-point error was "shared" between higher-than-expected variance resulting from over-fit weighting models, and overall bias, perhaps from polls having trouble modeling nonresponse or discerning which subgroups of the population were actually likely to vote.[16] All pollsters can come across variations on these problems regardless of how they process data.

In the end, the truth is not at either end of the spectrum of model-based and design-based polls, but at both ends simultaneously. The high-profile election misfires of the last decade prove that a good design is no silver bullet. But you cannot weight your way out of bad data. The best poll is one that selects its sample carefully and weights by enough variables to cut down on bias while not exploding its variance.

7

TAKING THE PULSE OF THE PULSE OF DEMOCRACY

> Voters in 2020 are well advised to regard election polls
> and poll-based prediction models with skepticism, to treat
> them as if they might be wrong and not ignore the cliché
> that polling can be more art than science. Downplaying
> polls, but not completely ignoring them, seems useful
> guidance, given that polls are not always in error.
>
> —W. JOSEPH CAMPBELL, *LOST IN A GALLUP*, 2020

When the sun peeked over the horizon on November 9, 2016, it did so over a world rocked to its core. Many felt as if the earth had been pushed into a new orbit. The *New York Times* plastered the headline TRUMP TRIUMPHS: OUTSIDER MOGUL CAPTURES THE PRESIDENCY, STUNNING CLINTON IN BATTLEGROUND STATES on its front page. London's *New Statesman* ran a cover story devoted to "The Trump Apocalypse." The *Daily Telegraph* of Sydney, Australia, opted for the crisper headline WHAT. THE. FUCK.

Donald Trump's victory was shocking not only because of his past—few had believed that the reality television star could win even the Republican primary for president, let alone the White House—but also because a mass of data suggested he would lose. Almost every public opinion poll showed Clinton with a robust lead nationwide and with a clear advantage in all the crucial swing states—Florida, Pennsylvania, Michigan, Wisconsin, and North Carolina—that he actually won, and underestimated his strength in the states that he was projected to win.

And it was not just the data gurus who underestimated Trump. Journalists had also brushed off his chances. Jamelle Bouie, the chief political correspondent for *Slate* in 2016, said in the summer, "There is no horse race here. Clinton is far enough ahead, at a late enough stage in the election, that what we have is a horse running by itself, unperturbed but for the faint possibility of a comet hitting the track. Place your bets accordingly."[1] He went on: "Clinton's odds of losing this election amount to the general chance of an unimaginable black-swan event that transforms the political landscape." Ryan Grim, who in 2016 was the Washington Bureau chief at the *Huffington Post*, even went so far as to accuse those forecasters who were less than 98% certain about the outcome of rigging their algorithms to deflate the probability of Clinton's victory. Three days before the election, Grim wrote, "If you want to put your faith in the numbers, you can relax. She's got this."[2]

Nobody who looked at the history of electoral success for candidates with as impressive a résumé as Hillary Clinton, or who was alarmed by Mr. Trump's indecency or clear unpreparedness for the office, could imagine him occupying the White House. According to Nolan McCaskill, a reporter for *Politico*, even Trump did not envision a victory.[3]

TWO DAYS AFTER THE 2016 ELECTION, the *New York Times* published a story titled "How Data Failed Us in Calling an Election." In it, technology journalists Steve Lohr and Natasha Singer chastised election

forecasters for getting the contest "wrong." They decried the media's growing reliance on data to handicap the horse race. "Data science is a technology advance with trade-offs," they wrote. "It can see things as never
before, but also can be a blunt instrument, missing context and nuance."
Lohr and Singer charged election forecasters and handicappers with taking their eyes off the ball, focusing on the data without considering other
sources for prognostication.[4]

Election forecasters, in turn, blamed the pollsters. But it was not only
the data that failed us in 2016, if indeed you want to call the performance
a "failure." It was faulty interpretation of that data—by the media, by
some forecasters, by academics and intellectuals, and, yes, by the public.
Still, polls did miss the outcome in 2016, and the pieces to that puzzle
have only recently fallen into place: after pollsters did even worse in 2020.

WEIGHT FOR IT

I called Charles Franklin as the sun began to set on a hot summer day in
2020. He answered from a book-filled room in his home in the suburbs
of Madison, Wisconsin—a state that had been key to Donald Trump's
2016 victory. We went through the blow-by-blow of election night, which
he spent at ABC headquarters on the "decision desk"—a group of nerds
who analyze vote returns and call states as results become clearer—and
discussed the various sources of error for his final poll of Wisconsin,
which had Hillary Clinton beating Donald Trump by six percentage
points, 46% to 40%. (In the end, Trump won by less than a point, 47.2%
to Clinton's 46.5%.)

Franklin believes that, more than anything, his error in Wisconsin
was due to a late-breaking shift toward Donald Trump among key undecided voters. Franklin's poll had stopped collecting data a week before
the election, giving ample time for fence-sitters to make up their minds in
favor of Trump. If Franklin's last poll was right, then there was a seven-

point swing to Trump in the last week of the campaign. He reckons that if he had conducted another poll a day or two before the election, he would not have missed this pivot to Trump.[5]

Franklin says that twenty percent of Wisconsinites had unfavorable views of both Trump and Clinton, and 75% of those ended up voting for Trump. According to exit polls, voters who decided who to vote for in the final week of the campaign picked Trump by a 29-point margin. The late-breaking shift was strongest in the suburbs. The Marquette poll under-estimated Trump's margin by 14 points in the Milwaukee suburbs and 7 points outside Green Bay. According to Franklin, "A lot of those suburban Republican voters had expressed reservations about Trump. But they also had very deep antipathy toward Hillary Clinton." In the end, their feelings about Clinton were simply too strong to be overcome by their reservations about Trump.[6]

To Franklin, the predictive errors in 2016 amount to "a failure of design, not of methodology." After Trump's victory, the Marquette poll resumed its typical respectable record. It predicted that the Democratic candidate for governor in 2018, Tony Evers, would win the election by a one-point margin. He won by 1.1. The same year, Franklin polled the Wisconsin Senate race at a 10-point margin for Democratic incumbent Tammy Baldwin—and she won by 11.

Franklin reckons he would have projected a closer race in Wisconsin if he had stayed in the field through Election Day, but he had reasons for releasing data before that. He says he believes surveys should be snapshots in time: tools for measuring public opinion, good for more than predicting the outcome of the horse race. He is interested in putting "information out into the world" while people can still use it. A poll of how many voters support farm subsidies is useless to politicians if it is released on Election Day; if they have it a week earlier, they might be motivated to support the popular position on the issue. For Franklin, the potential downside of missing a close contest that hinges on late deciders is less important in the grand scheme of things.

Charles Franklin is not the only pollster who faced a reckoning for his performance in 2016. In May 2017, the American Association for Public Opinion Research (AAPOR), the professional organization for pollsters, met in New Orleans to discuss the causes of, and fallout from, Trump's surprise election seven months earlier. There were no fewer than six different panels or presentations on the accuracy of pre-election polls. Most of these presented similar theories for the 2016 misfire.

To the extent that there was a systematic failure of pre-election polling in 2016, it was that some polls didn't survey enough white voters without college degrees, a group that tends to vote for Republicans. Educational attainment was a major predictor of presidential vote preference in the 2016 election, but many pollsters did not weight for it. An analysis by the *New York Times* found that nearly half of the respondents in a typical national poll had at least a bachelor's degree. But the percentage of college graduates among the actual population is only 28%. This presents a problem for pollsters who don't take the education of the electorate into account: because college-educated Americans are more likely to vote for Democrats, their unadjusted polls will overestimate support for Democrats.[7]

Some pollsters suffered badly from making this mistake in 2016. According to AAPOR's post-election report, the final University of New Hampshire poll had Clinton leading in the Granite State by 11 points. She ultimately won by a razor-thin 0.4-point margin. Andrew Smith, the director of the UNH poll, reported that they had adjusted their data for age, gender, and region, but not education. The combination had worked just fine in previous election cycles. He wrote:

> We have not weighted by level of education in our election polling in the past and we have consistently been the most accurate poll in NH (it hasn't made any difference and I prefer to use as few weights as possible), but we think it was a major factor this year. When we include a weight for level of education, our predictions match the final number.[8]

Other pollsters avoided making so egregious an error. Charles Franklin has weighted by education for his entire career. "It never dawned on me that polls would not be weighting by education," he told me, "not only for vote consequences, but because one of the strongest and longest-lasting trends in polling is that more educated people are more likely to respond to polls. I just took it for granted that you would weight for education."

Still, plenty of other pollsters missed the importance of education weighting. The *New York Times* reported shortly after the AAPOR conference that under a third of polls in battleground states included the variable in their adjustment protocols. In the Midwest, the percentages were even smaller; only 18% and 27% of surveys in Michigan and Wisconsin, respectively, had the right educational composition. Nate Cohn estimated that weighting by education would have improved the performance of polls by four percentage points.[9] AAPOR found slightly larger effects in Michigan, where a final poll from Michigan State University would have decreased Clinton's vote margin by seven points if it had been weighted to the share of educated voters in the population.[10]

ERRORS ON TOP OF ERRORS

By 2020, most political analysts thought that the pollsters had fixed the problems from the last go-around. About half of pollsters who didn't weight by education were weighting by it this time, and everyone knew (or should have) that large errors were possible.

But things didn't go much better for the pollsters in 2020. The outlier ABC/*Washington Post* poll that missed Joe Biden's margin by 17 percentage points in Wisconsin was called out as one of the biggest misses in the history of polling. It nearly gave the *Literary Digest* a run for its money. But the aggregates in Wisconsin were also off; Nate Silver's model had Biden up by eight points, when he only won by 0.6.

So while cherry-picking by focusing on outliers like the ABC/*Washington Post* poll is not fair to the pollsters, they are in some serious trouble. Worse, the polls in 2020 were off in all the same places they were in 2016, often by larger amounts. Whatever pulse the polls were taking in Ohio and Iowa, where forecasts were off by eight percentage points on average, was not the public's. Polls in Florida, often viewed as the ultimate swing state, were nearly five points off. Overall, these errors were 1.5–2 times as large as should be expected based on the historical margin of error of a state-level polling aggregate.[11]

Writing for the *Atlantic* the day after the election, David Graham characterized the results as "a disaster for the polling industry and for media outlets and analysts that package and interpret the polls for public consumption, such as FiveThirtyEight, the *New York Times*'s Upshot, and *The Economist*'s election unit. They now face serious existential questions."[12]

Graham's critique missed the mark in two important ways. First, it measured polling error the day after the election, when true results were not yet known; the polls began to look much better during the week after the election, as more Democratic-leaning ballots from big cities were counted. And by repeating the conventional wisdom about how polls "failed" to predict the 2016 and 2020 elections, he indulged in hyperbole. Pre-election polling was not perfect—polls rarely, if ever, are—but it was not catastrophically bad either.

Instead of being hopelessly broken, pre-election polls face severe and prolonged threats from partisan nonresponse. They are not reaching enough Republican voters. That's why polls underestimated Donald Trump in Wisconsin, and why the GOP candidate in Maine, Susan Collins, beat her polls in 2020 too. The precise reason for their lapse in numbers is harder to determine.

One theory, a holdover from the 2016 election, is that the voters who tend to be less trusting of their neighbors and government institutions are both less likely to answer polls and more likely to support Republicans for office, in ways that elude the variables that both traditional and twenty-first-century pollsters can account for.[13] A low-trust voter might be a 21-

year-old college-educated woman from Iowa now living in Philadelphia, or a 65-year-old Republican man in the Deep South. Low-trust voters tend to hide within aggregate statistics, biasing polls toward higher-trust people among all demographic groups. A poll that is not weighted to so-called social trust will miss this source of potential error.

Donald Trump's supporters may also have been more likely than their demographics predicted to refuse pollsters' calls because the president constantly railed against the pollsters, calling them corrupt and often alleging they were out to get him. This has never been a central theme in a presidential campaign before. After the election, Doug Rivers found that YouGov's polls often had too many rural voters in them, even after weighting by geography, and that people who voted for Mr. Trump in 2016 but disapproved of him in 2020 were more likely than his approvers to answer surveys.[14]

Pollsters also have the unenviable task of figuring out who is actually likely to turn up to vote on Election Day, and there is no agreed-upon method for predicting who is a "likely voter." Naïvely, we might think that pollsters could simply ask a person if they are likely to cast a ballot. But people lie, systematically saying they're more likely to vote than not, which throws the data out of whack.

Pollsters have to adjust for this, too, or their predictions will be off. They have toiled at the guesswork involved in anticipating Americans' real voting behavior since nearly the birth of modern survey research. Every pollster has a different method for predicting who will end up voting, and none offer definitive accuracy. (There's the Gallup method, the Perry-Gallup method, probabilistic vote-scoring, predictions from machine-learning models, the matching of vote-histories, and so on.) So ambiguous and uncertain are likely voter models that Burns "Bud" Roper, son of the public polling pioneer, said in 1984 that "one of the trickiest parts of an election poll is to determine who is likely to vote and who is not. I can assure you that this determination is largely art."[15]

The compound effects of weighting and filtering out nonvoters were so notable in 2016 that Nate Cohn arranged to have the *Times* proprietary data for a poll in Florida handed out to four different polling firms and groups of researchers to produce estimates using whichever method they preferred. Each pollster deployed defensible likely voter filters and performed standard weighting procedures to ensure samples were representative of the voting population by a mixture of age, sex, education, party registration, gender, and race.

In the end, the four polls—all based on exactly the same interviews—gave four different assessments of the race. One had Clinton up by four points, another by three, a third by one, and the fourth had Trump winning by a point.[16] But which made the "right" methodological choices? There is no way of knowing for sure. The divergence in their results is not necessarily proof that some methods are better than others, but rather a testament to the true potential for error in the polls. (The poll that had Trump winning Florida by a point was also not necessarily right, as it was taken in late September and the race could have changed between then and November.)

In the end, the lack of an accurate "standard likely voter" model may have led polls to overestimate support for Clinton. According to Cohn's polls in Florida, Pennsylvania, and North Carolina, Hillary Clinton's supporters were likelier than Donald Trump's to stay home after indicating their intention to vote. People who said they would vote favored the Democratic candidate by one point across the three states, but actual voters went for Trump by two.[17]

However, according to Nate Cohn, his operation at the *Times* managed rather good predictions of turnout for each party in 2020. Missing the "likely voter" explained only about one percentage point of his error in vote share. That wouldn't explain their nearly five-point error in Wisconsin or two-point miss in Michigan.

MOVING OFF THE GOLD STANDARD

David Shor, who now runs his own team of pollsters and analysts for progressive clients, believes that 2020 was even more of a warning of the impending death of traditional phone polling than 2016. In contrast to the previous election, when national polls were "very close to spot-on, there was a two percentage point bias on the presidency, and [the pattern in] state bias was identical to what it was in 2016." This suggests both that pollsters did not fix the underlying issues from 2016 and that something else got worse across the board.[18]

The causes of these errors were twofold, according to Shor. "First was overestimating support among non-college whites. Then there was a second error, due to coronavirus making Democrats stay at home," where they were more likely to answer a pollster's calls or fill out a survey online.

Eventually, the latter bias faded as people returned to work and pandemic-era public health measures were lifted. But the first bit of error will persist, in a way that weighting for education apparently did not fix. "And there will be another thing," Shor warns; there is always the possibility that something pollsters can't predict ahead of time will cause their polls to err. "Differential nonresponse is shockingly volatile," Shor says. "Take social trust: It used to be relatively uncorrelated with partisanship, and then in 2016 it was correlated with partisanship." Then, in 2020, coronavirus caused new problems. There is no way of adjusting for everything ahead of time.

Shor warns that the traditional RDD polling model, and phone polling in general, "has really fundamental problems. . . . People who answer phone surveys are much, much more politically engaged than the general population. And that's true even if you control for vote history." In other words, if you take two people with the same demographic traits and voting habits, and the only thing that separates them is that one answers a poll, the one who answers the poll will be more highly politically engaged—and in ways you can't control for. According to Shor, this also introduces partisan biases into polls. "Answering a survey is a political act that's super correlated with partisanship," he says. The people who didn't answer polls in 2020 could have been more Republican than the people who did answer in part because they just weren't as engaged in politics.

According to Shor, these problems are deep and fundamental and aren't easily fixed by the simple changes that people like to talk about. Response rates are too low; responding is too polarized. The only way to get around this is to use some sort of mixed-mode poll—to gather responses from both phone and online surveys, and maybe even by SMS text message—and train advanced machine learning algorithms to offer sophisticated controls for potential biases. The future of polling, according to Shor, is much more complex—and less transparent—than the polls of even the last decade. "The old model of polling, and of pollsters, where you have a polling shop and one or two political science grad students and you call a bunch of people, doesn't work anymore."

And some types of polls have recently performed worse than others. In one study, political scientists Peter K. Enns and Jake Rothschild aggregated 355 polls conducted between September 1 and November 1, 2020, and compared their accuracy by survey mode. The authors grouped the polls by whether the firm used probability, non-probability, or "mixed-mode" surveys. A good example of a probability poll is the ABC/*Washington Post* poll, which uses RDD to reach respondents. YouGov's online polls are considered non-probability because they aren't designed using samples of the full population; and a mixed-mode poll is one that combines data from two sources, such as Enns and Rothschild's own polls today (they combine a poll fielded via address-based sampling with data gathered over the web). They found that the polls conducted using mixed methods were much more accurate than the pure "probability" polls that use live interviewers to conduct the poll, often called the "gold standard" of survey research:

> Among surveys of likely voters (LV), probability-sample polls produced an average raw error of 6.1%, while non-probability samples were, on average, 2.5 percentage points more accurate, with a mean raw error of 3.6%. Mixed samples were more accurate still, with an average raw error of just 1.3%.[19]

Further, they found that RDD polls were not significantly more accurate than other types of probability polling, including polls that are conducted online but recruited via mail, such as the Pew Research Center's polling, and polls conducted off a voter file, such as the *New York Times*'s. The gold standard was not so golden after all.

WHAT POLLSTERS REALLY KNOW ABOUT POLITICS

At a conference hosted by Duke University in January 2021, researchers and pollsters from around the world met online to discuss the faults of their 2020 election polls and ways to fix surveys in the future. One problem they identified is that pollsters systematically overestimate their own accuracy. Courtney Kennedy, who assesses methodology at Pew, attested that the traditional margin of error that pollster reports is "fatally flawed." Because polls can be pushed in either direction by many factors beyond sampling error, she argued, pollsters should adopt a new standard for conveying the uncertainty in their data.[20]

Traditionally, regardless of whether they were conducting a preelection poll or a general survey of public opinion, pollsters have tended to report margins of error that only capture the uncertainty resulting from random deviations in sampling. That margin of error is calculated using a poll's sample size, with smaller polls having higher potential error than larger polls.[21] But this traditional margin of (sampling) error does not account for the potential for bias that can come from people not answering a call or filling out an online survey (which pollsters call nonresponse error), issues with question wording and response options that can influence respondents' answers (measurement error), whether or not the list from which samples are drawn includes an entry for each person in the population (coverage error), or other methodological choices such as the choice of weighting algorithm (or, for election polls, the way a pollster creates their likely voter filter). Worse, these are the extra sources of error that cause polling aggregates to be uniformly biased against certain responses.

The overwhelming majority of pollsters have failed to communicate these issues to the average political reporter, and newspapers have typically not included these caveats in their coverage of pollsters who have mentioned it.

To be sure, there is no easy solution. Pollsters do have a statistically sound way to measure the extra uncertainty introduced by the weighting adjustments they make to create more accurate polls. They call it the "design effect"—it is a measure of how much bigger the margin of error for their poll should be to take into account all the extra processing they do to a sample to bring its population estimates in line. But even the design effect is too small, only increasing the reported margin of error by about half in most cases.[22] In contrast, we have seen that the true margin of error for a poll is at least twice as large as the one for sampling error alone.

Once you account for all this extra uncertainty, it becomes tempting to argue that the polls did not perform *that* badly in 2016 or 2020. Indeed, it is clear that we should not expect hyper-accuracy from pollsters. But it is also reasonable to sound the alarm when they are regularly off in the same direction during election years; if we cannot rely on the polls to provide high-quality election predictions, can we rely on them to reliably produce other insights for our politics?

Many of our electoral and governing institutions are now influenced by polling. In the 2016 and 2020 elections, organizers of several presidential primary debates decided which candidates (out of some twenty choices on either side) to include in prime-time coverage, and whom to relegate to lesser-watched spots the next night. If polls underestimated support for one candidate, that may have had a direct impact on their electoral fortunes.

Similarly, as chapter 3 showed, politicians pay attention when polls tell them the public is behind them or against them. If the data our leaders are relying on are biased, they may be choosing to prioritize the wrong issues, or pursuing the wrong policies. This bias could influence both the president, who has massive power over the direction of the ship of state, and Congress, where members are constantly seeking a public mandate for reelection.

So, how good are the issue polls? Research on this front is reassuring. In March 2021, the Pew Research Center's methodology team looked at whether their 2020 polls of substantive issues—say, on health care, gun control, and economic stimulus—might have been inaccurate due to the same underlying causes that pushed their pre-election polls off course. Were they overrating support for universal health care by six percentage points as well? Were they underrating support for trade protectionism and Donald Trump's proposed wall along the US-Mexico border?

To answer this question, Pew took nine surveys that they conducted during the election year and re-weighted each of them so that the percentage of self-proclaimed supporters of Donald Trump and Joe Biden matched the actual results of the election. In effect, they created perfectly unbiased polls. Then, they created a separate set of "tilted "polls where Joe Biden's margin over Donald Trump was 12 points—an intentionally large number that would serve as an example of an extremely biased pre-election survey. This allowed them to compare support for various policies in the corrected polls to support in the "tilted" versions. They found that the vast majority of questions didn't display significant amounts of bias; the response options on forty-eight questions changed by less than half a percentage point, and the average bias toward the left-leaning answer was only one point. Polls of the general public—at least, those conducted by Pew—were largely safe from harm, they claimed.[23]

Finally, one study of issue polls in early 2021 by three political scientists and pollsters found that polls of state ballot initiatives between 1958 and 2020 did not systematically favor either conservatives or liberals.[24] The issues plaguing pre-election polling have not sunk the issue polls.

POLLING'S PERPETUAL MOTION

Though public opinion research is a science with a lot of precision, there are still many uncertainties. Conducting a good political poll relies on designing a good survey and correctly weighting the variables, most of which shift with each survey—and with each sample, each issue, and each election. It is unreasonable to expect polls to be crystal balls. Acknowledging all their sources of error is a starting point for considering how polling can in fact still be very useful (especially if polls are conducted the right way). Polls do not have to be electron microscopes to do what we want them to do.

But they do have to reach a minimum threshold of accuracy. By their own admission, pollsters took a harsh beating in 2016. In 2020, popular criticism gave the exaggerated impression that polls were on life support, cords sagging from the hospital bed as the tools used to measure the body politic lay besieged by various threats to the health of the industry. You would have thought from journalists' accounts that partisan nonresponse, low response rates, and margins of error that were too narrow had sent polls into a full-blown coma.

That picture is too harsh. On average, polls still do a reasonable job of informing the public debate on issues, and snapshots of electoral behavior are close enough to the true results to be better than most alternatives. Would we want to go back to sending out newspaper reporters to trawl the streets for enough willing participants to release straw polls before voting day? Or, as in 1824, having local militias call the roll? Given that the polls are our best chance at reading the tea leaves of public opinion, the fix for their role in journalism may lie, in part, on lowering our expectations for them.

It is also impossible to expect polls to progress linearly toward better methods and higher accuracy each year. Pre-election surveys are indeed in a worse state than they have been in a very long time. Until pollsters can figure out solutions to the problems they face, they will be looked upon skeptically by the public they seek to serve. While the future of polling looks bright, driven largely by research into online and mixed-mode polls, moving forward will require massive changes from the current status quo—both in methodology and in communication. Newer technologies might be harder to explain to readers and thereby decrease polling's value. Firms without the financial means or skill to make the transition could go out of business, or continue to pollute the information ecosystem with their bad data.

But since its invention, despite many perceived failures, political polling has persisted. The only option is for pollsters to try new things and move forward.

CONCLUSION

Public opinion sets bounds to every government, and is the
real sovereign in every free one.

—JAMES MADISON, FROM AN ESSAY FOR THE
NATIONAL GAZETTE, 1781

Public opinion polling might have ushered in a new era of democracy, if we had let it. Though no fans of Athenian democracy, many of America's founders were firm believers in the supremacy of the people and the majoritarian principle. By the late nineteenth century, a club of democrats had emerged who believed public opinion was, in the words of James Bryce, "the real ruler of America," but unfortunately society had not yet found the "machinery for weighing or measuring the popular will from week to week or month to month." Bryce hypothesized that "if the will of the majority of citizens were to become ascertainable at all times, and without the need of its passing through the body of representatives," then the American people could usher in a "fourth stage" of democracy.

Then, the public opinion—at least for the enfranchised white, male voters of the time—"would not only reign but govern."[1]

George Gallup and Saul Forbes Rae brought the United States one step closer to a government by public opinion. Voicing their utopian dream in *The Pulse of Democracy*, the authors outlined a vision of the United States in which a continual reassessment of the public's attitudes and priorities, a rolling referendum on the issues of government, might even render traditional republican governance obsolete. Why not cut out the intermediary—the elected representative—and go straight to the source of democracy itself: the people? An institution emulating a nationwide New England town hall would let the wisdom of the crowd decide the course of the government on any number of issues the pollsters felt free to inquire on.

The invention of a device to constantly survey the attitudes of the average citizen remade the way we think about our relationships to the government. Fundamentally, polls allowed those with a democratic spirit to finally obtain an answer to that pesky question that has plagued republicans since the birth of the nation: How can we ensure that the government is actually responding to the demands of its people?

THE ADVISORY REFERENDUM

Instead of a binding rolling referendum—which would likely have been an unwise step in American democracy, given what we have learned about the uncertainty in polling and the varying quality of public opinion across issues—we have arrived merely halfway to Gallup's utopia. Our current representative republic incorporates the insights of the polls mainly through a hyper-mediated information environment where a mainstream public poll is released and instantly covered in most major news outlets, parroted by journalists on social media, and compiled by congressional staffers for daily reports on news coverage and public pressures. Private polls may also be released by advocacy organizations and political campaigns themselves, exerting other corrective pressures on our leaders. The will of the people is now quantified and easily accessible by any reformer, legislator, or interested citizen.

Through the polls, the people have become willing participants in the democratic process. When they are called by a pollster, or fill out a survey online, they are implicitly engaging their elected officials in a representative act. Those who respond to a survey with approval of the actions of an elected official are voting for the status quo; those who oppose are participating in a miniature recall election. And they can sound off for and against any number of policies the government may be considering—or neglecting. These distributed town hall meetings are happening all over the country, many times per day, hundreds of times per year. This may not be the fourth stage that Bryce and Gallup foresaw. But it is still one realization of the power of the people through surveys.

At the same time, while the pollsters have been busy studying the numbers, a series of anti-democratic institutions and organizations have emerged in the United States. Interest groups, lobbyists funded by dark money, and demagogic politicians all play outsized roles in our politics— relative to their share of the population—and often move government policy away from the general will. Without polls, these forces could make claims about public opinion and manufacture inflated support for their policies—and we would have no way to correct them. Further, many scholars argue that because of the disconnect between preferences for policies, as uncovered by the polls, and the policies we get, the government is not as fully "representative" as it ought to be. One study by the political statisticians David Broockman and Christopher Skovron found that state legislators overestimated the popularity of conservative policies by as much as 20 percentage points on some issues. The authors concluded that "a novel force can operate in elections and in legislatures: Politicians can systematically misperceive what their constituents want."[2]

But even when they are not acting nefariously, politicians can be led away from the will of the people by biased measurements of public opinion. In 1863, during the Civil War, Abraham Lincoln held regular meetings in the White House with ordinary citizens. The people "representing all ranks and classes" would stand in a "grand waiting room," according to the political scientist Susan Herbst, and wait their turn to see the president. He was receptive to their commentary—so much so that New York journalist Charles Halpine remarked to Lincoln that Lincoln should install some sort of screening system to optimize his time spent talking to the average person. Lincoln responded negatively, conveying instead how they served a critical function in anchoring his rule to the will of the people.[3]

"No hours of my day are better employed than those which thus bring me again within the direct contact and atmosphere of the average of our whole people," Lincoln said. He believed that politicians and activists were apt to "become merely official" in their ideas and "with each passing day, to forget that they only hold power in a representative capacity." The remedy to the slow drift away from the people was to meet with them regularly, and to approach the engagement in good faith. "I call these receptions my 'public opinion baths,'" Lincoln remarked, "for I have little time to read the papers and gather public opinion that way; and though they may not be pleasant in all their particulars, the effect, as a whole, is renovating and invigorating to my perceptions of responsibility and duty."[4]

While Lincoln showed an admirable devotion to the public in this instance, a need to respond to their opinions, and a belief in their collective wisdom, his meetings hardly constitute a representative sample. But imagine, for a second, that you are Abraham Lincoln, and George Gallup has just walked into the Oval Office with a three-ring binder presenting his latest accurate reading of the public sentiment on the issues of the day. Such an advocacy would be more accurate and more populist in nature than Lincoln's surveying the opinions of only those men with the resources and gusto to journey across the country for a meeting with the president. The polls present a meaningfully less biased picture of opinion than the inherently elitist circles of politicians, lobbyists, and leaders who otherwise make contact with our elected officials.

Without polls, government policy—and the public itself—would be at high risk of corruption by the informational and ideological warfare that has become typical of modern politics. Donald Trump's presidency presented more than a glimpse of what an authoritarian could accomplish if we lacked any information about what the public really wanted. Throughout his tenure in office, Trump claimed to represent the "true" will of the people, despite losing the popular vote twice and routinely proposing unpopular policies. Two days after the 2020 election, when things began to look very bad for him, the president held a press conference and derided the polls as being purposefully biased against his silent majority of voters: "The pollsters got it knowingly wrong," Trump said, "it was [voter] suppression polling, everyone knows that." In the months that followed, he pursued a fraudulent case against the results of the election, claiming—contrary to polls or vote counts—that the public opinion was actually behind him, that the people wanted him to implement his agenda instead of his competition's. He did all of this with the power and privilege that comes from the Oval Office. Polls gave small-"d" democrats an objective basis for correcting his misinformation.

American electoral institutions, supposedly designed to represent the will of the people, also frequently block their way. This is true even after the ratification of the Thirteenth, Fourteenth, and Twentieth Amendments to the Constitution, as well as the 1964 Civil Rights Act and 1965 Voting Rights Act, which gave political rights to women and Americans of color. Because both chambers of Congress and the United States presidency are elected based on a system of geographic representation—the House of Representatives with congressional districts that stretch from cities into the heartland, the Senate and Electoral College based on states with vastly different sums of people—they are at risk of being gamed by one party that performs better in rural areas than in cities. In recent memory, the Republican Party has tended to be that party. Since 2010, its comparative edge in the Electoral College has grown ever more severe. In the 2020 election, Republicans could have won the presidency while losing the popular vote for president by four percentage points—upward of 6–7 million votes, depending on turnout. The Republican Party has a slightly smaller structural advantage in the US House, where it can win with a three-point deficit. In the US Senate, meanwhile, Republicans have not won the popular vote across the three election cycles leading up to 1998 (the Senate is elected in thirds each two years, meaning popular-vote tallies must be done across three separate cycles), yet they have controlled the majority of seats in the chamber after seven of twelve congressional election cycles. In such a country, the minority of voters can routinely overpower the "will of the people" in the halls of government.[5]

Polls can help us here by highlighting the mismatch between what the people want from their government and what they actually get. The quantification of the will of all people can nudge politicians and activists toward the broader, more general public opinion, even when that opinion seems out of step with the party line. Richard Nixon pursued environmentalism, nuclear energy, and a withdrawal from Vietnam in part because his pollsters said it was politically expedient. Bill Clinton focused on child health care for the same reason. Donald Trump was also motivated by public support for criminal justice reform to join with Democrats and pass the 2018 First Step Act, one of the most popular actions of his presidency.

We are reminded again of that famous quote from Sidney Verba: "Surveys produce just what democracy is supposed to produce—equal representation of all citizens"; they are "designed so that each citizen has an equal chance to participate and an equal voice when participating."[6] As there are numerous ways in which the will of the people is distorted as it makes its way to and through the levels of government, a person must see polls as only more necessary to the democratic experiment, not less.

MAKING POLLS WORK (AGAIN)

The polls have had some big misfires, but they are still the best tools we have to gauge support for the actions of the government. If the accuracy of polling overall is measured by the predictive abilities of election polls, then they are typically off by one percentage point here and two there, and the person in the lead ends up winning. Studies of issue polls directly suggest they may be more accurate than their pre-election counterparts.

More importantly, a one- or two-point miss is not nearly large enough to alter conversations about public policy. What is the practical difference between a position that is supported by 60% versus 62% of adults? Certainly the two-point difference would not change any politician's mind when so clear a majority has already decided in favor. And how much does the difference between even 48% and 50% matter? The latter is closer to a majority, but with both numbers within the margin of error of it, few leaders would be persuaded to do something risky just on the back of the single poll. On the whole, the picture of the country as uncovered by polls appears quite accurate.

This does not mean that all polls are good. We have seen how pollsters in Iraq and other overseas (particularly Middle Eastern) countries in the early twenty-first century struggled with the methods and business of survey-taking—or may have been influenced by authoritarian governments—and produced unreliable data that was likely even falsified. Those findings were passed up the chains of command to leaders in both the United Kingdom and United States—and distributed to the media. Along with so-called push pollsters, ideologically motivated firms, and attention-seekers, these examples remind us that we cannot fully let down our guard when gathering data on the will of the people, as we have seen how, across the board, not all polls are created equal.

Over the ninety-year history of polling, we have learned public opinion surveys are less like pulse oximeters and more like a cracked mirror—a tool that reveals a portrait of the gazer that is roughly correct, but with notable imperfections. These cracks became apparent after polls were faulted for very real methodological shortcomings during elections in both the recent and distant past—but also by routine and unfair beatings by critics who do not understand either the science behind them or their value to democracy. Though the reflective surface can sometimes offer up a distorted view of the American public, we have seen that its imperfections do not render it absolutely useless. Luckily, unlike a glass mirror, the polls can be fixed to a large degree, cracks filled and blemishes polished out. Pollsters are constantly engaging in the process of repair, but citizens too can help polling regain its footing and realize its full potential. Ultimately, the fixes will lead us to ask ourselves: Can we use the mirror to improve our democracy?

I PROPOSE FIVE REFORMS that pollsters, political practitioners, the media, and the public can adopt to elevate the polls. First, pollsters should abandon polls fielded entirely by phone, and incorporate samples drawn by other methods. Due to the rise of caller ID and other call-blocking technologies, as well as a general distrust of the pollsters, phone polling has become increasingly unreliable and incredibly expensive. Phone pollsters face a deadly combination of high costs due to the labor demands of dialing additional cell phone numbers by hand, and a lack of high-quality population benchmarks to which they can adjust their samples to ensure their representativeness, especially by demographic group. There was a time when over 90% of people you called would answer a phone poll; now, pollsters are lucky to get five or six percent of people to tell them how they feel and what they think. And that group is unrepresentative.

While pure phone polls have been trending toward irrelevance, online pollsters have been proving their worth. Through experimentation with new data-collection methods and innovations in statistics, firms such as YouGov and Civiqs have outperformed pure "probability" methods that performed well in the past. Their ability to gain repeated observations from the individuals over time enables them to produce samples that are often more politically representative than a phone poll fielded among a random subset of the population. The firms using Erin Hartman's method of adjusting for predicted nonresponse, like David Shor's and the *New York Times*, have also developed powerful ways to adjust their samples to be better representative of the population. At the very least, they do not miss elections by 17 points.

Pollsters also ought to invest in more off-line methods, such as the address-based methods that the Pew Research Center developed during the 2020 election. These methods should help pollsters derive higher-quality population benchmarks for things like partisanship, religious affiliation, and trust in our neighbors—data that can be used to adjust other polls and improve the landscape of public opinion research. Benchmarking surveys could also be completed in conjunction with the government, which still manages to get very high shares of people to fill out its census surveys, or through a commercial partnership that distributes the benchmarks to its partner organizations. While these methods might not fix the underlying problem with polls—certain groups of people refusing to answer their phones or fill out online surveys at rates standard modeling has a hard time capturing—they will go a long way toward repairing them.

Second, pollsters should be open to the fact that their opinion polls are subject to roughly twice the potential error that is captured by the traditional margin of sampling error—and political journalists should treat individual surveys with more skepticism. A pre-election poll that shows one candidate leading by two or three points should not be treated as a solid poll for that candidate, or even a sign that they are leading. If there is a two-point spread and a six- or seven-percentage-point margin of error, you are only slightly better off betting in favor of the leading candidate; the bet would not be safe—and so journalists should report the contest as a toss-up. At the very least, the press should always report the margin of error of a poll near the top of the story. Smarter journalism would remind readers and listeners of the many different factors that could cause the survey to go wrong.

Accordingly, and third, election forecasters should revisit their old ideas about the ability of aggregation to remove biases in a mass of data, and their ability to convey the likelihood of those biases to readers. The savants have had two contests in a row where they badly underestimated one candidate across states. The first time, Donald Trump won enough extra votes to win the Electoral College and overcome his poor 15–30% chance of victory in the leading models; the second time, his vote share in two states was higher than in 80–90% of simulations forecasters generated. In the future, it could be wise for forecasters to reframe their commentary as exploring what could happen if the polls go wrong, rather than providing pinpoint predictions of the election. The expectations of hyper-accuracy, largely caused by the media's misunderstanding of Nate Silver's successful forecasts in 2008 and 2012, as well as his championing of correct forecasts in binary terms, but to which I have contributed as well, should be consigned to the history books. Forecasting should become an enterprise for exploring uncertainty, not predicting outcomes.

Fourth, to combat the influence of low-quality outfits that are motivated by profits or ideology, the American Association for Public Opinion Research (AAPOR) ought to more aggressively and publicly sanction public pollsters who do not release thorough, transparent reports on their methodologies. Additionally, when a survey firm is suspected of faking its data or engaging in other nefarious activity, AAPOR should investigate it and engage in additional high-profile scrutiny—both to incentivize good behavior and to shore up public trust in the industry. Instead of being a professional society for the pollsters, AAPOR could transform itself into a public watchdog for survey data. If it publicly condemned the practices of ideologically biased or nefarious firms, thereby affecting news coverage and client recruitment to produce a loss of revenue for bad actors, AAPOR could cut down on the number of unsavory outlets at home, clean up the public opinion information environment, and restore trust in the industry.

Finally, to better achieve the promise of polls in a republican government, more political interest groups should devote themselves to measuring and advocating for the public's opinions. Data for Progress, a progressive think tank that was started in 2018, has data-driven advocacy at the core of its mission. Their secret is a combination of speed, accuracy, and networking. The nerdy progressives who run the group's polls use a cheap online survey platform called Lucid to field quick surveys with large amounts of respondents, often running multiple questionnaires simultaneously. Then, the methodologists weight their data to be both politically and demographically representative—as per the breakdowns of the voter file—and an army of authors write quick reports and publish them online. While a traditional media poll will take weeks to design, field, weight, and report, Data for Progress can ask the questions it needs and publish the findings in a matter of days.

The business model works. For example, for months during 2018, politicians and many in the media claimed that a package of climate policies called the "Green New Deal" would drag down Democrats in swing districts. But Data for Progress released a report using polling and MRP modeling showing strong support for the policy in swing districts. The report was tweeted out by the bill's cosponsors, New York representative Alexandria Ocasio-Cortez and Massachusetts senator Ed Markey, reaching millions of people, and was covered extensively in the media, including an exclusive in *Vox*. In early 2020, the founder of Data for Progress, Sean McElwee, landed a meeting with Joe Biden's political team and may have pushed his advisors to put climate policy at the forefront of the campaign. The group even convinced New York senator Chuck Schumer, the Senate majority leader, to blog on the firm's website in support of unemployment insurance, which it found was very popular. "We've developed a currency that [politicians] are interested in," McElwee told the *New York Times* in 2021. "We get access to a lot of offices because everyone wants to learn about the numbers."[7]

Poll-based public interest groups do not have to be advocacy-focused. They can partner with newspapers to share their findings and still meaningfully improve the political discourse. In the summer of 2021, for example, the Republican Party engaged in a full-throated campaign against critical race theory (CRT), a body of legal scholarship about racism and racial inequalities developed in the late twentieth century. Several Republican-led states, including Texas and Florida, banned coursework that talked about CRT or related subjects (such as the *New York Times*'s 1619 Project, a series of articles that examines the country's history from the date when enslaved people first arrived on American soil). But a poll conducted by YouGov and published in partnership with *The Economist* found that only 26% of Americans had even heard "a lot" about CRT, and fewer had a clear idea of what it was. What misconceptions about their aggregate attitudes and priorities would the American people have held if those polls were not published?

Fielding timely and relevant polls can point legislators toward the things the people actually care about. If they don't address key issues, or enact policies that a majority doesn't like, the people can use the data to hold their leaders to account. In our fourth stage of democracy, the press, advocacy groups, and constituents would all work together to facilitate the link between the government and the governed—by using the polls.

Together, these steps would help fix the methods, correct the misconceptions, and elevate the impacts of public opinion polling in America. But do not mistake these prescriptions for polls as promises of democracy. A higher pedestal for the polls will not fix the many other forces working against representative government. I do not promise that polls are a panacea. Still, if we are interested in living under a truly representative government, more and better polling at least pushes us in the right direction.

We, the people, hold the final key to unlocking polling's future. When the pre-election pollsters do make their next misstep, when some inevitably fall on the wrong side of 50-50 during the next election, we should not throw the baby out with the bathwater. We should remember that political polling is more like a weather prediction than a medical instrument; that the margin of error, at least twice as big as the one pollsters and journalists report, does not assign binary outcomes to elections but rather detects the probable distribution of opinions among the population. We should remember that aggregation and modeling do not remove the chance for all polls to be biased in the same direction. We must internalize the vision of polls as indicating a range of potential outcomes for an election, ballot initiative, or constitutional referendum, rather than a hyper-accurate point-prediction. Polls were not invented to produce such a thing—and due to the statistical laws of survey sampling and the complexities of psychology and human behavior, they never will.

DEMOCRACY'S LOOKING GLASS

These suggestions constitute a real paradigm shift in how we use and evaluate the polls. We should think of public opinion surveys primarily as tools for a better democracy, and only secondarily as election forecasts—which were largely developed to prove the validity of polls anyway.

Over the last century, public opinion polls have been woven into the very fabric of American democracy. Some people have characterized this relationship as a damaging one, but the evidence suggests otherwise. Political polls give us the ultimate yardstick to measure the quality of our government. If a poll declares an elected leader's performance to be dramatically out of step with the people's wishes, then, armed with objective evidence and numerical authority, we are empowered to demand immediate change. If the leader ignores our demands, we have empirical grounds to persuade other constituents to throw them out when they're up for reelection.

Polls are the ultimate corrective to the biases of our democratic institutions and the anti-majoritarian forces of lobbyists, monied special interests, and demagogues. That corrective is even more important between election years, when the people have no formal check on those in power. Elected leaders are supposed to flow with the currents of democracy, the demands of the people in aggregate, especially when their voice is united. The people should use polls to demand that politicians listen to them—both on their specific preferences and on their elucidation of the problems they face. The loss of the polling industry would be a tremendous setback for democracy. Without the polls, people who are marginalized from the political process—noncitizens, who still have rights to representation in the Constitution, and voters in uncompetitive states or districts—are left effectively voiceless in a political process that often strays from their desired path, pursuing the preferred policies of wealthy donors, corporations, and the most privileged classes. Critics of election polling and forecasting should direct their energies toward improving polling, not eliminating it.

In a country that promises to provide a government of, by, and for the people, polls are not just forecasts of the next election—they are a necessary and empowering addition to the democratic experiment. Public opinion polls serve as the mirror of a body politic. That mirror is cracked, but it is the best, the most reflective, one we have.

ACKNOWLEDGMENTS

I developed most of my writing abilities as a journalist. Writing a book presented very different challenges. Details must be fuller, narratives richer, structure clearer, and arguments made more explicitly, step by step. And this is my first book. As such, I have relied on many others in order to produce a work that is engaging, educational, and complete.

First, thank you to my parents, Mama and Poppo, to whom this book is dedicated, and to my wife, Taryn, who planned most of our wedding between reviewing drafts of these chapters and providing feedback on the cover. Thank you to my brothers and sister, as well as their families, for giving me their genuine reactions to the many iterations of this book's title and helping to point me in the right direction.

Thank you to my colleagues Jon Fasman and Kenn Cukier for reading the first draft of my book proposal and throwing it out. If this book is good, it is a reflection of many things you taught me about writing. (If it is bad, I take full responsibility.) Thank you to my bosses at *The Economist* for granting me leave to finish this book after a restless election year in 2020.

Thank you to my literary agent, Lisa Adams, who helped me shape and sell the book when it was little more than a pile of scattered thoughts.

Thanks also to everyone at W. W. Norton who helped design and publish this book, especially my editors Quynh Do, who first bought the proposal, and Matt Weiland, who took over the project while it was still in its infancy. Thank you also to Gayle Rogers, who provided several rounds of edits for structural and organizational matters for no apparent reason other than he was interested and wanted to.

Thank you also to the many scholars and journalists who gave interviews for this book or on background material, including Mark Blumenthal, Charles Franklin, Yair Ghitza, Erin Hartman, Natalie Jackson, Courtney Kennedy, Steve Koczela, Drew Linzer, Doug Rivers, Michael Robbins, David Shor, Michael Spagat, and those left anonymous. Many others provided useful general feedback for the book; in particular, thank you to Scott Keeter, Carlos Algara, Andrew Gelman, and Jonathan Robinson (who also helped with chapter titles).

Thanks to my several academic mentors for their instruction and insight, much of which sparked my interest in writing this book. To those who reviewed drafts of my manuscript, thank you for doing that too. Christopher Wlezien taught me a great deal about public opinion, polls, and elections. Thank you to Bethany Albertson for teaching me about survey research methods, and for being a good friend. Thanks to Maraam Dwidar, E. J. Fagan, Bryan Jones, and Sean Theriault for teaching me research skills. I give my special thanks to the University of Texas Department of Government for providing library access and research support by appointing me to a faculty research position in 2020. Libraries are an invaluable resource. We should elect politicians who fund them and support administrators who open access to them.

Due to the nature of this book, I have come to rely heavily on secondary sources to supplement my own analyses and research, and to borrow theories and ideas that have been circulating for generations. These scholars will find their names in the text and chapter notes, but many deserve special recognition as this book comes to a close. That list includes (but is certainly not limited to) Adam Berinsky, Jean Converse, George Gallup, Susan Herbst, Sarah Igo, Simon Jackman, Scott Keeter, Courtney Kennedy, V. O. Key Jr., Jill Lepore, Christian Meier, Frank Newport, Vincent Price, Robert Shapiro, and Michael Traugott. The history of representative government is now thousands of years old, and polls, nearly a hundred. In that time, many thinkers doubtless contributed to the intellectual shape of these topics without contributing directly to the works detailed in these pages. These unmentioned scholars have my deep appreciation—as does anyone who feels they have been wrongly excluded from this list. I offer you a mention in the closing pages of my next book as a remedy. Or a beer.

Finally, I extend my heartfelt thanks to anyone who picked up this book at their local bookseller (or added it to their shopping cart online). Just as the people are the true sovereign in any state, so too are they the constituents for any successful author. I offer my final thanks to all of my readers.

NOTES

INTRODUCTION

1. Will Jennings and Christopher Wlezien, "Election Polling Errors across Time and Space," *Nature Human Behavior* 2, no. 4 (April 2018): 276–82.

2. David Rothschild and Sharad Goel, "When You Hear the Margin of Error Is Plus or Minus 3 Percent, Think 7 Instead," *New York Times*, October 5, 2016, https://www.nytimes.com/2016/10/06/upshot/when-you-hear-the-margin-of-error-is-plus-or-minus-3-percent-think-7-instead.html.

3. Meredith Heagney, "Justice Ruth Bader Ginsburg Offers Critique of Roe v. Wade During Law School Visit," University of Chicago Law School, May 25, 2013, accessed March 20, 2021, http://www.law.uchicago.edu/news/justice-ruth-bader-ginsburg-offers-critique-roe-v-wade-during-law-school-visit.

4. Justin McCarthy, "U.S. Support for Same-Sex Marriage Matches Record High," Gallup, June 1, 2020, https://news.gallup.com/poll/311672/support-sex-marriage-matches-record-high.aspx.

5. John W. Kingdon, *Congressmen's Voting Decisions* (New York: Harper & Row, 1973), 32.

CHAPTER 1: DEMOCRACY AND THE PUBLIC WILL

1. As cited by Scott Keeter, "Public Opinion Polling and Its Problems," in *Political Polling in the Digital Age*, ed. Kirby Goidel (Baton Rouge: Louisiana State University Press, 2011), 28–53.

2. James Madison, "For the *National Gazette*, [ca. 19 December] 1791," Founders Online, National Archives, https://founders.archives.gov/documents/Madison/01-14-02-0145. (Original source: *The Papers of James Madison*, vol. 14, *6 April 1791–16 March 1793*, ed. Robert A. Rutland and Thomas A. Mason [Charlottesville: University Press of Virginia, 1983], 170.)

3. "James Madison to Unknown, re Majority Governments, December 1834," Founders Online, National Archives, https://founders.archives.gov/documents/Madison/99 -02-02-3066.

4. "Thomas Jefferson to Annapolis Citizens, 1809," in *The Writings of Thomas Jefferson, Memorial Edition*, vol. 16, ed. Andrew A. Lipscomb and Albert Ellery Bergh (Washington, DC: Thomas Jefferson Memorial Association, 1903), 337.

5. Tunis Wortman, *A Treatise Concerning Political Enquiry, and the Liberty of the Press* (New York: Printed by George Forman, 1800), 118–19, 122–23, 155–57.

6. James Bryce, *The American Commonwealth* (Indianapolis: Liberty Fund, 1995). Originally published in 1888.

7. Bryce, *American Commonwealth*, 1174–81.

8. James Bryce, "Thoughts on the Negro Problem," *The North American Review* 153, no. 421 (1891): 641–60.

9. Andrew Whitby, *The Sum of the People: How the Census Has Shaped Nations, from the Ancient World to the Modern Age* (New York: Basic Books, 2020), 28.

10. Gary Urton, *Inka History in Knots: Reading Khipus as Primary Sources* (Austin: University of Texas Press, 2017), 179–80. As quoted in Whitby, *Sum of the People*, 29.

11. Whitby, *Sum of the People*, 30.

12. A. B. Wolfe, "Population Censuses before 1790," *Journal of the American Statistical Association* 27, no. 180 (1932): 357–70, DOI: 10.1080/01621459.1932.10502239.

13. Whitby, *Sum of the People*, 36.

14. "Athenaeus: The Deipnosophists," book 6, 262–75, trans. C. D. Yonge, 1854, http:// www.attalus.org/old/athenaeus6d.html#272.

15. Andrew Whitby, "We Still Need the Census to Tell Us Who We Really Are," *The Conversation*, September 24, 2013, https://theconversation.com/we-still-need-the-census -to-tell-us-who-we-really-are-18575.

16. Christopher W. Blackwell, "Athenian Democracy: A Brief Overview," in Adriaan Lanni, ed., *Athenian Law in Its Democratic Context* (Center for Hellenic Studies Online Discussion Series); republished in C. W. Blackwell, ed., *Dēmos: Classical Athenian Democracy*, The Stoa Consortium, February 28, 2003, https://www.stoa.org/demos/ article_democracy_overview@page=1&greekEncoding=UnicodeC.html.

17. Blackwell, "Athenian Democracy," 6.

18. Blackwell, "Athenian Democracy," 6.

19. Each deme was placed in a "third" according to its regional type: city, coastal, or countryside. There were ten of each third. Then, thirds were split into ten tribes in such a way that each tribe held a portion of a third from each region—Tribe 1, for example, would have one set of demes from each type of third, ensuring a mix of citizens from all three regions of the country. Each tribe then "elected" (by casting lots) 50 citizens to the Council of 500. In this way, the body was made up of representatives who could, in theory, satisfy the general needs and wants of all Athenians. For more, see Aristotle, *Aristotle in 23 Volumes*, vol. 20, *Athenian Constitution*, trans. Harris Rackham (Cambridge, MA: Harvard University Press, 1952), chapter 21, section 24.

20. Blackwell's explanation follows:

> Aristotle tells us that "There is a chairman of the presidents, one man, chosen by lot; this man chairs for a night and a day—no longer—and cannot become chairman a second time." This chairman kept the keys to the treasuries and archives of Athens, as well as the state seal. . . .
>
> It is worth noting that because there were 354 days in the legislative year more than two thirds of all Councilors would serve as chairman for a night and a day in a given year.
>
> There are further implications, if we accept the estimate of two scholars that in 400 BCE there were approximately 22,000 adult male citizens. . . .
>
> A citizen had to be 30 years old to serve as a Councilor. For the sake of argument, we might assume that the average citizen would then have an active political life of 30 years, until he was 60. During that time, there would need to be approximately 10,000 chairmen, each controlling the state seal and the treasuries, and presiding over the presidents of the Council for a day and a night. Since no one could serve as chairman twice, this office would have to go to 10,000 different Athenians. It follows, then, that approximately one half of all Athenian citizens would, at some point during their lives, have the privilege and responsibility of holding this office, arguably the closest equivalent to a Chief Executive in the Athenian democracy. (Blackwell, "Athenian Democracy," 6)

21. Plato, *The Republic*, book 8, sections 557–64, from *Plato in Twelve Volumes*, vols. 5 and 6, *The Republic*, trans. Paul Shorey (Cambridge, MA: Harvard University Press; London: William Heinemann Ltd., 1969), http://www.perseus.tufts.edu/hopper/text?doc=Perseus%3Atext%3A1999.01.0168%3Abook%3D8%3Asection%3D557c.

22. Plato, *The Republic*, book 4, section 424, http://www.perseus.tufts.edu/hopper/text?doc=Perseus%3Atext%3A1999.01.0168%3Abook%3D4%3Asection%3D424a.

23. Nikolaus Jackob, "Cicero and the Opinion of the People: The Nature, Role and Power of Public Opinion in the Late Roman Republic," *Journal of Elections, Public Opinion and Parties* 17, no. 3 (2007): 293–311.

24. Jackob, "Cicero and the Opinion of the People," 293–311.

25. As quoted in David W. Minar, "Public Opinion in the Perspective of Political Theory," *Western Political Quarterly* 13, no. 1 (March 1990).

26. John Locke, *Two Treatises of Government*, ed. Peter Laslett (New York: Mentor Books, 1963), section 149.

27. Leo Damrosch, *Jean-Jacques Rousseau: Restless Genius* (New York: Houghton Mifflin, 2005), 304.

28. Jean-Jacques Rousseau, *The Social Contract and Discourses* (London: J. M. Dent & Sons, 1920), 48.

29. "From James Madison to Benjamin Rush, 7 March 1790," Founders Online, National Archives, https://founders.archives.gov/documents/Madison/01-13-02-0062. (Original source: *The Papers of James Madison*, vol. 13, *20 January 1790–31 March 1791*, ed. Charles F. Hobson and Robert A. Rutland [Charlottesville: University Press of Virginia, 1981], 93–94.)

30. Walter Lippmann, *The Phantom Public* (New York: Transaction Publishers, 1925), 28.

31. Lippmann, *The Phantom Public*, 10.

32. Michael X. Delli Carpini and Scott Keeter, *What Americans Know about Politics and Why It Matters* (New Haven, CT: Yale University Press, 1996).

33. Christopher H. Achen and Larry M. Bartels, *Democracy for Realists: Why Elections Do Not Produce Responsive Government* (Princeton, NJ: Princeton University Press, 2016).

34. John Dewey, *The Political Writings*, ed. Debra Morris and Ian Shapiro (Cambridge, MA: Hackett Publishing Company, 1993), 197.

35. Philip E. Converse, "The Nature of Belief Systems in Mass Publics," in David E. Apter, ed., *Ideology and Its Discontents* (New York: The Free Press of Glencoe, 1964); and Jon A. Krosnick, "Government Policy and Citizen Passion: A Study of Issue Publics in Contemporary America," *Political Behavior* 12 (1990): 59–92.

36. Aristotle, *The Politics*, trans. T. A. Sinclair (London: Penguin Books, 1962), 123.

37. Iain Couzin et al., "Uninformed Individuals Promote Democratic Consensus in Animal Groups," *Science* 334, no. 6062 (December 16, 2011): 1578–80.

38. Benjamin I. Page and Robert Y. Shapiro, *The Rational Public: Fifty Years of Trends in Americans' Policy Preferences* (Chicago: University of Chicago Press, 2010), 385.

39. V. O. Key Jr., *Public Opinion and American Democracy* (New York: Alfred A. Knopf, 1961), 7.

40. E. E. Schattschneider, *The Semisovereign People: A Realist's View of Democracy in America* (New York: Holt, Rinehart and Winston, 1960), 134–36.

41. F. Rosen and J. H. Burns, eds., *The Collected Works of Jeremy Bentham: Constitutional Code*, vol. 1 (Oxford: Oxford University Press, 1983), 35–39; and T. P. Schofield, ed., *The Collected Works of Jeremy Bentham* (Oxford: Clarendon Press, 1990), 121.

42. Samuel Kernell, *Going Public: New Strategies of Presidential Leadership*, 4th ed. (Washington, DC: CQ Press, 2007), 112.

43. Lippmann, *The Phantom Public*, 21.

CHAPTER 2: POLLING COMES OF AGE

1. Tom W. Smith, "The First Straw? A Study of the Origins of Election Polls," *Public Opinion Quarterly* 54, no. 1 (Spring 1990): 24.

2. Smith, "The First Straw?": 26.

3. Smith, "The First Straw?": 26.

4. Smith, "The First Straw?": 29–30.

5. Patricia Cline Cohen, *A Calculating People: The Spread of Numeracy in Early America* (Chicago: University of Chicago Press, 1982), 206–7.

6. Claude Robinson, *Straw Votes: A Study of Political Prediction* (New York: Columbia University Press, 1932), 49.

7. Robinson, *Straw Votes*, 4.

8. George Gallup and Saul Forbes Rae, *The Pulse of Democracy: The Public-Opinion Poll and How It Works* (New York: Simon & Schuster, 1940), 38.

9. Gallup and Rae, *Pulse of Democracy*, 38.

10. Robinson, *Straw Votes*, 50.

11. Robinson, *Straw Votes*, 58.

12. Archibald Crossley, "Straw Polls in 1936," *Public Opinion Quarterly* 1, no. 1 (January 1937): 27–28.

13. Sharon L. Lohr and J. Michael Brick, "Roosevelt Predicted to Win: Revisiting the 1936 *Literary Digest* Poll," *Statistics, Politics and Policy* 8, no. 1 (2017): 65–84.

14. "They Never Will Be Missed," *New York Times*, November 6, 1936, https://nyti.ms/2KDLOhI.

15. Gallup International Association, "George Gallup: Highlights of His Life and Work," accessed September 14, 2020, https://www.gallup-international.com/wp-content/uploads/2017/10/George-Gallup-Biography-22.pdf.

16. Gallup International, "George Gallup: Highlights," 7.

17. Gallup International, "George Gallup: Highlights," 8.

18. Gallup International, "George Gallup: Highlights," 13.

19. "George H. Gallup, Founder, 1901–1984," Gallup, accessed September 1, 2020, https://www.gallup.com/corporate/178136/george-gallup.aspx.

20. J. Michael Hogan, "George Gallup and the Rhetoric of Scientific Democracy," *Communication Monographs* 64, no. 2 (1997): 161–79.

21. Gallup's forecast—55.7% of the vote for Roosevelt and 44.3% for Landon—was also quite imperfect. However, his error margin amounted to 6.8 percentage points, while the *Digest* missed support for Roosevelt by closer to 20 points. Other pollsters, such as Archibald Crossley (53.8% for Roosevelt) and Elmo Roper (61.7%), also beat the *Digest*, proving the legitimacy of scientific sampling once and for all.

22. Gallup International Association, "Polling around the World" (Zurich, 2017), 89, https://www.gallup-international.com/fileadmin/user_upload/publications/Gallup-English-Book-2017.pdf .

23. Gallup International Association, "Polling," 89.

24. David McCullough, *Truman* (New York: Simon & Schuster, 1992), 657.

25. McCullough, *Truman*, 657.

26. Gallup International Association, "Polling," 93.

27. W. Joseph Campbell, *Lost in a Gallup: Polling Failure in U.S. Presidential Elections* (Oakland: University of California Press, 2020), 82.

28. Campbell, *Lost in a Gallup*, 62.

29. Campbell, *Lost in a Gallup*, 5.

30. Frederick Mosteller, Herbert Hyman, Philip J. McCarthy, Eli S. Marks, and David B. Truman, *The Pre-Election Polls of 1948* (New York: Social Science Research Council, 1949), viii.

31. Campbell, *Lost in a Gallup*, 82.

32. Campbell, *Lost in a Gallup*, 82.

33. Morris L. Ernst and David Loth, *The People Know Best: The Ballots vs. the Polls* (Washington, DC: Public Affairs Press, 1949), 117.

34. Adam J. Berinsky, "American Public Opinion in the 1930s and 1940s," *Public Opinion Quarterly* 70, no. 4 (Winter 2006): 507.

35. Sarah E. Igo, *The Averaged American* (Cambridge, MA: Harvard University Press, 2007), 132.

36. Joel T. Campbell, Leila S. Cain, Anatol Rapoport, and Philip E. Converse, "Public Opinion and the Outbreak of War," *Journal of Conflict Resolution* 9, no. 3 (1965): 318–33.

37. The statistical "Law of Large Numbers" maintains that repeated sampling from a target population will converge around the average attribute after a certain sample has been obtained, depending on the distribution of opinions of that sample, if selection and response are truly randomized.

38. Campbell, *Lost in a Gallup*, 84.

39. Paul Perry, "Election Survey Procedures of the Gallup Poll," *Public Opinion Quarterly* 24, no. 3 (Autumn 1960): 531–42.

40. Irving Crespi, *Pre-Election Polling: Sources of Accuracy and Error* (New York: Russell Sage Foundation, 1988), 42.

41. Crespi, *Pre-Election Polling*, 30.

42. Bryce, *American Commonwealth*, 929.

43. Gallup and Rae, *Pulse of Democracy*, 290.

44. Lindsay Rogers, *The Pollsters: Public Opinion, Politics and Democratic Leadership* (New York: Alfred A. Knopf, 1949), 69.

45. Rogers, *The Pollsters*, 92.

46. Rogers, *The Pollsters*, 17.

47. George Gallup, "A Reply to *The Pollsters*," *Public Opinion Quarterly* 13, no. 1 (Spring 1949): 179–80.

48. Vincent Price and Peter Neijens, "Opinion Quality in Public Opinion Research," *International Journal of Public Opinion Research* 9, no. 4 (Winter 1997): 336–60.

CHAPTER 3: MACHINE POLITICS

1. Jill Lepore, "Are Polls Ruining Democracy?," *The New Yorker*, November 8, 2015, https://www.newyorker.com/magazine/2015/11/16/politics-and-the-new-machine.

2. Jill Lepore, *If Then: How the Simulmatics Corporation Invented the Future* (New York: Liveright, 2020), 192.

3. Sidney Hyman, "If Computers Called the Tune," *New York Times*, June 28, 1964, https://www.nytimes.com/1964/06/28/archives/if-computers-called-the-tune-the-480-by-eugene-burdick-313-pp-new.html.

4. Melvin Holli, *The Wizard of Washington: Emil Hurja, Franklin Roosevelt, and the Birth of Public Opinion Polling* (New York: Springer, 2002), 18. My account of Hurja is taken primarily from this source.

5. Holli, *The Wizard of Washington*, 42–43.

6. Holli, *The Wizard of Washington*, 42–43.

7. Holli, *The Wizard of Washington*, 42–43.

8. Holli, *The Wizard of Washington*, 53–54.

9. Robert M. Eisinger and Jeremy Brown, "Polling as a Means toward Presidential Autonomy: Emil Hurja, Hadley Cantril and the Roosevelt Administration," *International Journal of Public Opinion Research* 10, no. 3 (1998): 12.

10. Holli, *The Wizard of Washington*, 62.

11. Holli, *The Wizard of Washington*, 62.

12. Holli, *The Wizard of Washington*, 63.

13. Holli, *The Wizard of Washington*, 66.

14. Holli, *The Wizard of Washington*, 67.

15. Holli, *The Wizard of Washington*, 68.

16. Holli, *The Wizard of Washington*, 65.

17. Holli, *The Wizard of Washington*, 70.

18. Holli, *The Wizard of Washington*, 73.

19. Holli, *The Wizard of Washington*, 88.

20. Holli, *The Wizard of Washington*, 110–19.

21. Holli, *The Wizard of Washington*, 82.

22. Lepore, *If Then*, 192.

23. Lepore, *If Then*, 92.

24. Lepore, *If Then*, 103; and Ithiel de Sola Pool, Robert P. Abelson, and Samuel Popkin, *Candidates, Issues, and Strategies: A Computer Simulation of the 1960 Presidential Election* (Cambridge, MA: MIT Press, 1965), 43.

25. See Paul F. Lazarsfeld, Bernard Berelson, and Hazel Gaudet, *The People's Choice: How the Voter Makes Up His Mind in a Presidential Campaign* (New York: Columbia University Press, 1948). A second study was conducted in Elmira, New York (thus dubbed the "Elmira Study"). See also Bernard Berelson, Paul F. Lazarsfeld, and William N. McPhee, *A Study of Opinion Formation in a Presidential Campaign* (Chicago: University of Chicago Press, 1954).

26. Pool, Abelson, and Popkin, *Candidates*, 9–11.

27. Lepore, *If Then*, 110; Pool, Abelson, and Popkin, *Candidates*, 97.

28. Lepore, *If Then*, 119.

29. Lepore, *If Then*, 121.

30. Pool, Abelson, and Popkin, *Candidates*, 21–22.

31. Michael Wheeler, *Damn Lies and Statistics: The Manipulation of Public Opinion in America* (New York: Liveright, 1974), 49–51.

32. Wheeler, *Damn Lies and Statistics*, 51–52.

33. Lawrence R. Jacobs and Robert Y. Shapiro, "Issues, Candidate Image, and Priming: The Use of Private Polls in Kennedy's 1960 Presidential Campaign," *American Political Science Review* 88, no. 3 (September 1994): 531–35.

34. Lepore, *If Then*, 142.

35. Lepore, *If Then*, 126.

36. Lawrence R. Jacobs and Robert Y. Shapiro, "The Rise of Presidential Polling: The Nixon White House in Historical Perspective," *Public Opinion Quarterly* 59, no. 2 (Summer 1995): 165–67.

37. A full list is available in Jacobs and Shapiro, "The Rise of Presidential Polling," 168, fn12.

38. Jacobs and Shapiro, "The Rise of Presidential Polling," 172–76.

39. Jacobs and Shapiro, "The Rise of Presidential Polling," 189.

40. Jacobs and Shapiro, "The Rise of Presidential Polling," 191.

41. Jacobs and Shapiro, "The Rise of Presidential Polling," 183–84.

42. Jacobs and Shapiro, "The Rise of Presidential Polling," 179–80.

43. Wheeler, *Damn Lies and Statistics*, 15.

44. Robert Y. Shapiro and Lawrence R. Jacobs, "Source Material: Presidents and Polling: Politicians, Pandering, and the Study of Democratic Responsiveness," *Presidential Studies Quarterly* 31, no. 1 (March 2001): 159.

CHAPTER 4: ONE BAD APPLE DOESN'T SPOIL THE BUSHEL

1. Igo, *The Averaged American*, 128.

2. Michael Spagat, "Truth and Death in Iraq under Sanctions," *Significance* 7, no. 3 (September 2010): 116–20.

3. According to global data from UNICEF, the under-five mortality rate in 2019 was 37.7 deaths per 100,000, while the neonatal rate was 17.5 per 100,000. United Nations Interagency Group for Child Mortality Estimation (UN IGME), "Under-Five Mortality," August 2021, https://data.unicef.org/topic/child-survival/under-five-mortality/.

4. Spagat, "Truth and Death," 119.

5. Tony Blair, "Rt Hon Tony Blair Transcript, The Iraq Enquiry, Oral Evidence," National Archives, January 29, 2010, https://webarchive.nationalarchives.gov.uk/ukgwa/20171123123237/http://www.iraqinquiry.org.uk//media/45139/20100129-blair-final.pdf, 243–44.

6. Michael Spagat, "Ethical and Data-Integrity Problems in the Second *Lancet* Survey of Mortality in Iraq," *Defense and Peace Economics* 21, no. 1 (April 2010): 19.

7. The US Broadcasting Board of Governors—a government agency, now called the US Agency for Global Media, which operates several media outlets in foreign countries to further "US national interests"—hired KA Research to conduct the poll. See Michael Spagat, "Evidence of Potential Fabrication in Iraq Public Opinion Polls from 2005–2008," unpublished paper, 3.

8. Spagat, "Evidence of Potential Fabrication," 3.

9. Spagat, "Evidence of Potential Fabrication," 3, and an interview with the author on October 25, 2021.

10. Spagat, "Evidence of Potential Fabrication," 3.

11. The 2011 paper was not published until Spagat himself posted it online in 2016. When, years earlier, the paper had been submitted for publication in a journal, one of the companies involved threatened to sue Spagat, Koczela, and the institutions with which they were affiliated if the paper was published. When Spagat finally published the paper in 2016, an executive with that company told the *Huffington Post* that the company had gone "the legal route" because Spagat and Koczela had sent their findings to the company's clients before sending it to the company. "Why did it go to our clients first if the concern was to open a discussion about data fabrication issues?" the executive report-

edly asked. For more, see Natalie Jackson, "Emmy-Winning Iraq Polls May Have Been Tainted by Fabrication, Researchers Say," *Huffington Post*, March 18, 2016, https://www .huffpost.com/entry/Iraq-polls-fabrication_n_56ecb215e4b03a640a6a945b.

12. Spagat, "Evidence of Potential Fabrication," 7.

13. Spagat, "Evidence of Potential Fabrication," 13. The correlation between questions for suspect supervisors was -0.04; for others, it was 0.37.

14. Michael Spagat, "More Evidence of Fabrication in D3 Polls in Iraq, Part 1: War, Numbers and Human Losses," May 24, 2016, https://mikespagat.wordpress.com/2016/05/24/ more-evidence-of-fabrication-in-d3-polls-in-iraq-part-1/.

15. Regina Faranda, director of the OPN, and State press officials, interviews with the author, March–April 2021.

16. Langer Research Associates, "Reply to Spagat," March 31, 2016, https://www .langerresearch.com/wp-content/uploads/Reply-to-Spagat_3-31-16.pdf.

17. Michael Spagat, interview with the author, February 2, 2021.

18. Michael Dimock, "Data Quality Deserves an Honest Discussion," Pew Research Center, February 24, 2016, https://www.pewresearch.org/methods/2016/02/24/data -quality-deserves-an-honest-discussion/.

19. Mollie J. Cohen and Zach Warner, "How to Get Better Survey Data More Efficiently," *Political Analysis* 29, no. 2 (2021): 121–38.

20. "Push Polling," *The Colbert Report*, January 17, 2008, video, https://www.cc.com/ video/otl5ul/the-colbert-report-push-polling.

21. Mike Huckabee disavowed the independent group responsible for this push polling. See: "Huckabee Disavows Misleading Campaign Tactics," *NPR Morning Edition*, January 16, 2008, https://www.npr.org/templates/story/story.php?storyId=18138859.

22. Richard Gooding, "The Trashing of John McCain," *Vanity Fair*, November 2004, https://www.vanityfair.com/news/2004/11/mccain200411.

23. Gooding, "Trashing of John McCain."

24. Gooding, "Trashing of John McCain."

25. Nate Cohn, "There's Something Wrong with America's Premier Liberal Pollster," *New Republic*, September 12, 2012, https://newrepublic.com/article/114682/ppp-polling -methodology-opaque-flawed#footnote-114682-$2

26. Harry Enten and Nate Silver, "Why Did a Rasmussen Reports Poll Disappear?," FiveThirtyEight, October 24, 2014, https://fivethirtyeight.com/features/why-did-a -rasmussen-reports-poll-disappear/.

27. G. Elliott Morris, "Are Pollsters Herding Their Polls of the 2020 Democratic Primary?," September 1, 2019, https://gelliottmorris.substack.com/p/september-1-2019 -are-pollsters-herding.

28. Fran Coombs, "The Liars Say We're Outliers—Again," Rasmussen Reports, April 17, 2018, https://www.rasmussenreports.com/public_content/politics/commentary_by_ fran_coombs/the_liars_say_we_re_outliers_again.

29. Andrew Gelman, "Estimated House Effects" (Biases of Pre-election Surveys from Different Pollsters) and Here's Why You Have to Be Careful Not to Overinterpret Them,"

Statistical Modeling, Causal Inference, and Social Science, October 19, 2020, https://
statmodeling.stat.columbia.edu/2020/10/19/estimated-house-effects-biases-of-pre
-election-surveys-from-different-pollsters/.

30. Zack Stanton, "'People Are Going to Be Shocked': Return of the 'Shy' Trump Voter?," *Politico,* October 29, 2020, https://www.politico.com/news/magazine/2020/10/29/2020-polls-trump-biden-prediction-accurate-2016-433619.

31. Fox News, "Pollster Predicts a Trump Victory for 2020 Election," *Sunday Morning Futures with Maria Bartiromo,* November 2, 2020, https://video.foxnews.com/v/6206222587001#sp=show-clips.

CHAPTER 5: AMERICA IN AGGREGATE

1. Sean Jeremy Westwood, Solomon Messing, and Yphtach Lelkes, "Projecting Confidence: How the Probabilistic Horse Race Confuses and Demobilizes the Public," *Journal of Politics* 82, no. 4 (October 2020).

2. Mark Blumenthal, "Polls, Forecasts, and Aggregators," *PS: Political Science and Politics* 47, no. 2 (April 2014): 1.

3. Blumenthal, "Polls, Forecasts, and Aggregators."

4. Charles Franklin, interview with the author, February 3, 2021.

5. Mark Blumenthal, interview with the author, February 3, 2021.

6. Blumenthal, interview, February 3, 2021.

7. Nate Silver, "General Election Projections, Beta Version," *Daily Kos,* February 26, 2008, https://www.dailykos.com/stories/2008/2/26/464643/-General-Election-Projections-Beta-Version.

8. Nate Silver (@natesilver538), "Today is the 10-year anniversary of http://FiveThirtyEight.com! Can't believe I've been doing this for a decade now. Thanks to y'all for reading and here's to 10 more years ahead," Twitter, March 7, 2018, https://twitter.com/natesilver538/status/971422777235226624?lang=en.

9. Natalie Jackson, interview with the author, March 2, 2021.

10. Matthew Yglesias, "James Comey Admits That His Read of the Polls May Have Influenced His Handling of the Clinton Email Probe," *Vox,* April 13, 2018, https://www.vox.com/2018/4/13/17233600/james-comey-weiner-emails.

11. Philip Tetlock, *Expert Political Judgment: How Good Is It? How Can We Know?* (Princeton, NJ: Princeton University Press, 2005), 134.

CHAPTER 6: BIG DATA AND BLACK BOXES

1. Sasha Issenberg, "How Obama's Team Used Big Data to Rally Voters," *MIT Technology Review,* December 19, 2012, https://www.technologyreview.com/2012/12/19/114510/how-obamas-team-used-big-data-to-rally-voters/.

2. Erin Hartman, interview with the author, March 9, 2021.

3. Hartman, interview, March 9, 2021.

4. Issenberg, "How Obama's Team Used Big Data to Rally Voters."

5. Author's estimates.

6. Author's analysis of likely voter modeling in publicly released polls.
7. Douglas Rivers, interview with the author, March 26, 2021.
8. "Privacy Online: Fair Information Practices in the Electronic Marketplace," Federal Trade Commission, May 2000, https://www.ftc.gov/sites/default/files/documents/reports/privacy-online-fair-information-practices-electronic-marketplace-federal-trade-commission-report/privacy2000text.pdf.
9. Michael Lewis, "The Two-Bucks-a-Minute Democracy," *New York Times Magazine*, November 5, 2000, https://archive.nytimes.com/www.nytimes.com/library/magazine/home/20001105mag-democracy.html.
10. Rivers, interview, March 26, 2021.
11. Yair Ghitza, "Applying Large-Scale Data and Modern Statistical Methods to Classical Problems in American Politics," PhD diss., Columbia University, 2014, 2.
12. Nate Cohn, "Projections Before the Polls Close: What Could Possibly Go Wrong?," *New York Times*, November 7, 2016, https://www.nytimes.com/2016/11/08/upshot/you-may-need-a-strong-stomach-for-the-pitfalls-of-real-time-election-projections.html.
13. Yair Ghitza, interview with the author, April 1, 2021.
14. For more on this dichotomy, see Nate Cohn, "Without wading into this specific debate…," February 3, 2020, Twitter.com, https://twitter.com/Nate_Cohn/status/1224421118976634882?s=20.
15. Nate Cohn, "How One 19-Year-Old Illinois Man Is Distorting National Polling Averages," *New York Times*, October 12, 2016, https://www.nytimes.com/2016/10/13/upshot/how-one-19-year-old-illinois-man-is-distorting-national-polling-averages.html2016.
16. Shirani-Mehr Houshmand, David Rothschild, Sharad Goel, and Andrew Gelman, "Disentangling Bias and Variance in Election Polls," *Journal of the American Statistical Association* 113 (2018): 522: 607–14.

CHAPTER 7: TAKING THE PULSE OF THE PULSE OF DEMOCRACY

1. Jamelle Bouie, "There Is No Horse Race," *Slate*, August 24, 2016, https://slate.com/news-and-politics/2016/08/there-is-no-clinton-trump-horce-race.html.
2. Ryan Grim, "Nate Silver Is Unskewing Polls—All of Them—in Trump's Direction," *Huffington Post*, November 5, 2016, https://www.huffpost.com/entry/nate-silver-election-forecast_n_581e1c33e4b0d9ce6fbc6f7f.
3. Nolan McCaskill, "Trump Tells Wisconsin: Victory Was a Surprise," *Politico*, December 13, 2016, https://slate.com/news-and-politics/2016/08/there-is-no-clinton-trump-horce-race.html.
4. Steve Lohr and Natasha Singer, "How Data Failed Us in Calling an Election," *New York Times*, November 10, 2016, https://www.nytimes.com/2016/11/10/technology/the-data-said-clinton-would-win-why-you-shouldnt-have-believed-it.html.
5. Charles Franklin, interview with the author, July 23, 2020.
6. "Exit Polls 2016," CNN, November 9, 2016, https://www.cnn.com/election/2016/results/exit-polls/wisconsin/president.

7. Nate Cohn, "A 2016 Review: Why Key State Polls Were Wrong about Trump," *New York Times*, May 31, 2017, https://www.nytimes.com/2017/05/31/upshot/a-2016 -review-why-key-state-polls-were-wrong-about-trump.html.

8. "An Evaluation of 2016 Election Polls in the U.S.," American Association for Public Opinion Research (AAPOR), 2017, https://www.aapor.org/Education-Resources/ Reports/An-Evaluation-of-2016-Election-Polls-in-the-U-$2aspx.

9. Cohn, "A 2016 Review."

10. AAPOR, "An Evaluation of 2016 Election Polls."

11. Author's estimates.

12. David Graham, "The Polling Crisis Is a Catastrophe for American Democracy," *The Atlantic*, November 4, 2020.

13. David Shor, interview with the author, February 17, 2021.

14. Douglas Rivers, interview with the author, March 26, 2021.

15. Burns W. Roper, "Political Polls: Some Things That Concern Me," remarks to the American Association for the Advancement of Science (May 25, 1983), Box 11, Roper papers, Thomas J. Dodd Research Center, University of Connecticut.

16. Nate Cohn, "We Gave Four Good Pollsters the Same Raw Data. They Had Four Different Results," *New York Times*, https://www.nytimes.com/interactive/2016/09/20/ upshot/the-error-the-polling-world-rarely-talks-about.html.

17. Cohn, "A 2016 Review."

18. Author's reporting. See G. Elliott Morris, "The Future of Public Opinion Polling," February 19, 2021, https://gelliottmorris.substack.com/p/cornell-belcher-polling -should-not.

19. Peter K. Enns and Jake Rothschild, "Revisiting the 'Gold Standard' of Polling: New Methods Outperformed Traditional Ones in 2020," *Medium*, March 18, 2021, https://medium.com/3streams/revisiting-the-gold-standard-of-polling-new-methods -outperformed-traditional-ones-in-2020-451650a9ba5b.

20. Author's notes. Courtney Kennedy, "Insights from Public Opinion Polling on the Future of Surveys," presentation at the Future of Survey Research Conference, Duke University, January 2021.

21. The typical formula is to take the square root of $[(0.5 * 0.5)/n]$ and multiply by 1.96, where n is the number of respondents and 1.96 represents the z-score for calculating a 95% confidence interval of a normal distribution.

22. Gary Langer, "Sampling Error: What It Means," ABC News, October 8, 2008, https:// abcnews.go.com/PollingUnit/sampling-error-means/story?id=5984818.

23. Scott Keeter, Nick Hatley, Arnold Lau, and Courtney Kennedy, "What 2020's Election Poll Errors Tell Us about the Accuracy of Issue Polling," Pew Research Center, March 2, 2021, https://www.pewresearch.org/methods/2021/03/02/what-2020s-election-poll -errors-tell-us-about-the-accuracy-of-issue-polling/.

24. Jonathan Robinson, Christopher Warshaw, and John Sides, "When Mass Opinion Goes to the Ballot Box: A National Assessment of State Level Issue Opinion and Ballot Initiative Results," 2021, unpublished.

CONCLUSION

1. James Bryce, *American Commonwealth*, 919.
2. David E. Broockman and Christopher Skovron, "Bias in Perceptions of Public Opinion among Political Elites," *American Political Science Review* 113, no. 2 (March 2013): 542–63.
3. Abraham Lincoln, "My 'Public-Opinion Baths,'" in Mario Cuomo and Harold Holzer, eds., *Lincoln on Democracy* (New York: HarperCollins, 1990), 284–85; as cited in Susan Herbst, *Numbered Voices: How Opinion Polling Has Shaped American Politics* (Chicago: University of Chicago Press, 1993), 173.
4. Herbst, *Numbered Voices*, 173.
5. Stephen Wolf, "How Minority Rule Plagues the Senate," *Daily Kos*, February 23, 2021, https://www.dailykos.com/stories/2021/2/23/2013769/-How-minority-rule-plagues-Senate-Republicans-last-won-more-support-than-Democrats-two-decades-ago.
6. Keeter, "Public Opinion Polling and Its Problems," 28.
7. Lisa Lerer, "Born on the Left, Data for Progress Comes of Age in Biden's Washington," *New York Times*, June 12, 2021, https://www.nytimes.com/2021/06/12/us/politics/data-for-progress-democrats.html#click=https://t.co/1Zip5RWeFK.

INDEX

Page numbers beginning with 182 refer to endnotes.